Delivering Good Youth Work

A Working Guide to Surviving and Thriving

Gina Ingram and
Jean Harris

University of Chester Library
Tel: 01925 534284

Russell House Publishing

First published in 2001 by:
Russell House Publishing Ltd.
4 St. George's House
Uplyme Road
Lyme Regis
Dorset DT7 3LS

Tel: 01297-443948
Fax: 01297-442722
e-mail: help@russellhouse.co.uk

British Library Cataloguing-in-publication Data:
A catalogue record for this book is available from the British Library.

ISBN: 1-898924-97-X

Typeset by The Hallamshire Press Limited, Sheffield.
Printed by Cromwell Press, Trowbridge

Russell House Publishing

Is a group of social work, probation, education and youth and community work practitioners and academics working in collaboration with a professional publishing team. Our aim is to work closely with the field to produce innovative and valuable materials to help managers, trainers, practitioners and students. We are keen to receive feedback on publications and new ideas for future projects.

To Steve and Owen for forbearance beyond the call of duty

Contents

Introduction

If you work with young people, full or part time, paid or voluntary, this book is for you!

How many times have you heard youth workers say something like:

> *What keeps me in the job is the young people...they drive me mad but they make me laugh...I get such a buzz when one of them does something that shows that they're growing up...It's fantastic when they achieve something beyond your wildest dreams. After all this time, it still makes me feel great because I've done something that really counts...*

> *...paperwork, hassle and no recognition: that's the real downer. I know its all got to be done, but there's so much, and it hangs over me and gets me down...I don't work as well as I want to and that's depressing in itself.*

> *...No one can tell you how to cope, you must learn what works for you...What you do need is lots of support...in all these changes, that seems to have gone. We work in far more isolated situations than ever before* (Vickty, experienced part time worker)

This book is about coping, surviving and thriving in order to work more effectively with young people. It is about dealing with the issues that Vickty describes, using a range of techniques including planning and delivering high quality youth work, the management of yourself and others and working with other agencies.

We have also placed workers' experiences in a wider context:

- Theory
  The right amount of appropriate theory often helps you to think through and analyse what is happening. It enables you to make effective plans for action to help your work with young people.
- The social, political and economic background
  We live and work in a world of change. All of us are affected by changes that occur at local, regional, national, international level. Examples of this include changes in the systems of benefit, transport and health. These factors affect young peoples' lives too. Youth workers must be aware of these changes so that they can help young people cope; and to be able to speak out for, and with, them on their issues.

The aims of the book

This book is based on workers' experiences and their feelings about them. It aims to provide insight to help you analyse your situation and to:

- Understand the forces acting on the lives of the young people you work with.
- Be able to identify their needs.
- Plan strategically and develop action plans.
- Design, deliver, monitor and evaluate work to meet their learning needs.

- Reflect on your work and learn from your experience.
- Build your credibility by recording and publicising your work.
- Manage yourself, your staff and your managers.
- Identify how other organisations work and understand your own organisation.
- Work effectively with management committees and steering groups.
- Build and maintain an effective youth forum and advocate on behalf of young people and the service.

In the process of doing this, the book develops strategies for coping, surviving and thriving as a worker in order to deliver more effective youth work:

- time management
- boundary management
- stress management
- building a support network

The World of Change

The only constant thing is change.   (Anon)

Here are a few recent examples which affect all our lives:

- Movement in employment away from heavy industries and towards the service and IT industries.
- Technology and the information revolution.
- The 24 hour society.
- 'Fast' foods.
- Drugs and illegal substances more readily available.
- Decline in the nuclear family.
- Decline in membership of organised religions.

These social, political and economic changes impact on:

- The young people we work with.
- Us, as members of communities, families and as individuals.
- The organisations we work for.

Youth workers need to be aware of these changes and how they affect young people's lives in order to:

- Advocate on their behalf.
- Inform managers so that youth work is developed in a way that is relevant and appropriate to the young people's needs.
- Keep our own practice current.

These changes cause pressures on young people which makes the process of growing up more difficult. Some young people do not adjust well to these pressures and are harder to work with and more demanding.

Organisations that employ youth workers are themselves under pressure. For example changes in funding, Health and Safety, Child Protection and the introduction of Best Value and the Connexions Service all require organisational responses. This means that, more and more, people have to learn to work in a different way.

The Government policy of 'joined up thinking' means that youth work is now carried out by a range of agencies such as social services, health authorities and schools. People carrying out this work may not have been trained as youth workers. The effect of this is that there is often less common understanding of what good youth work might be and more difficulties in working with other agencies.

Many local authority youth services as we knew them are shrinking, as are some voluntary youth organisations. As funding regimes change, there are more short term projects and consequently workers with short term contracts. This work is often tightly targeted and driven by the need to achieve measured outcomes. In principle this is good practice, however if the outcomes are not achievable or the workers feel that they are diverted from meeting the needs of the young people, then the process is extremely frustrating. Those workers that have to continually seek short term contracts find that:

- Their lives lack stability.
- Their professional development is often stunted.
- The projects often cease because of change in or lack of funding rather than for professional reasons.

For those on long term contracts, there is often a mismatch between the needs of the communities in which they work and the available funding. Further there is often pressure to seek external funding for what was previously mainstream work.

All of these changes put further pressure on youth workers.

The Kipper Effect

You, the face to face youth worker works under difficult conditions. There are pressures from all sides: the result of these pressures can be that the youth worker who started as a well rounded person gets squashed flatter and flatter. In the words of the old joke, they finish up like a kipper. As everyone knows, a kipper has no backbone, is flat (one dimensional) and looks both ways at once! This book will help you avoid being 'kippered'.

What are the forces that cause 'kippering'?

Youth Work: A Definition

Given this fluid and pressurised situation we felt that it was important to be clear about the component parts of good youth work. When you are clear about what you are doing and how you undertake it you are in a position to:

- analyse and develop your practice
- describe and market your work

both of these are 'anti-kipper' techniques.

Youth work is a learning process in which:

- Youth workers and young people come together voluntarily.
- The youth worker forms a caring, equal relationship with the young people.

The purpose of this relationship is to provide a context in which:

- The young person's learning needs can be identified.

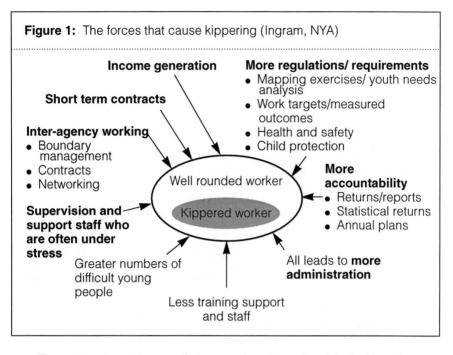

Figure 1: The forces that cause kippering (Ingram, NYA)

- The needs are met in a way that moves them towards achieving the autonomy to take control of their lives in a responsible way.

The learning is offered:
- In a safe climate within a framework of equality of opportunity.
- In a participative, planned and evaluative way.

…and is relevant, appropriate and fun for each individual or group of young people. The worker assists the young people to move towards independent adult lives.

The general increase in demands placed on workers comes from a number of factors outlined above, all of which produce more administrative pressures. In order to be an effective worker, you need to understand the factors which are 'kippering you' and employ strategies to deal with them (see table below).

Factors	Strategies
Young people are becoming increasingly more demanding to work with.	Understanding their situation. Analysing their needs Designing programmes which meet their needs. Annual planning. Recording, monitoring and evaluating the work.
Supporting and managing others.	Being an effective manager.

Staff development.
Line management and supervision.

A wider and more demanding job description. Time management.

Boundary management.

Short term contracts.

Stress management.
Support frameworks.
Assertiveness and saying 'no'.

The general increase in demands placed on workers:
 - income generation
 - inter-agency work
 - increased administration
 - working to targets

Having a clear vision of the work.
Building your credibility by recording and publishing successes.
Reflecting on your work and learning from your experiences.
Understanding your organisation.
Understanding service level agreements and frameworks of agreement.
Managing your manager.
Working with management committees and steering groups.
Building and maintaining effective youth forums.

Chapters 1, 2, 3 provide an analysis of why we are being 'kippered': the rest of the book looks at practical, real and workable anti-kipper strategies.

As you read this book be critical and keep asking:

- Is this my reality?
- How do I feel about this?
- How do I modify and develop this analysis to make it relevant to my work and the lives of the young people I work with?

This book is a tool, use it as such. This means that you should take, modify and develop the ideas according to your needs. Pass your successful thoughts and methods on to others. The process of sharing and developing ideas is what has kept field work relevant to young people in a changing world. It is also why the field has always led the way in the development of good practice. Be part of that process…

Jean Harris has a wide experience of working with young people, including running an SRB project and Duke of Edinburgh's Award Schemes in London and Doncaster. She has undertaken a number of roles for the Doncaster Metropolitan Borough Council's Youth Service, and currently manages a Connexions team of personal advisers.

Since **Gina Ingram** qualified as a youth worker in 1972, she has been involved in youth work as a field worker, manager, trainer and consultant. Throughout this time she has been concerned with the growth and development of young people and youth workers.

Chapter One

Young People in Today's Society

I'm really glad I'm not a kid now...I don't know how they cope with it...well, some of them don't, do they? (Parent of children, 7, 13 and 15 years old, Liverpool)

When you work with a relatively small number of hard-to-help young people, it is sometimes easy to get dispirited and feel that nothing you do makes any difference.

I've tried...you wouldn't believe how I've tried. I've listened to them for hours. We've planned things that they wanted to do and then half of them don't turn up. When you ask them why, they say 'it's boring' and worse: but they've not even tried it!

Some things we plan together, half of them join in, but the rest just destroy it. I've banned some and the others beg me to let them back in. As individuals they are OK, as a group I can't cope. I've tried everything I know...it must be me.

(Dorset youth worker)

If you have ever felt like this, it may help to realise that you are not alone. When you consider the social situation of young people you can see the wider problems with which you are working.

We hope that this chapter will help you in that:

- It may help you stay motivated and sane.
- You can use this analysis to explain to others (other professionals; management committees; decision makers) why youth work is so difficult and demanding at the moment.
- You can also use it to analyse your own working situation, making planning and decision taking easier.
- It can be used as the basis of a case to argue for more resources.
- The analysis should help when you are advocating for and with young people. It should act as a secure base from which to make your case.

An Analysis of the Social Situation of Young People

A group of full and part-time workers from Blackpool were exploring the world in which they lived with the young people with whom they worked. In a few minutes they pooled their findings and collectively produced Figure 2 below.

They had not explored the area before and they rapidly realised that their work demonstrated two important points:

1. Young people's lives are very complex and growing up in the UK today can be very difficult.

2. Youth workers need to hold a huge range of information and regularly update it in order to work effectively with young people. Keeping up with the changes in the law, the development of agencies and services, and being aware of funding bodies that are relevant to young people are major tasks in themselves.

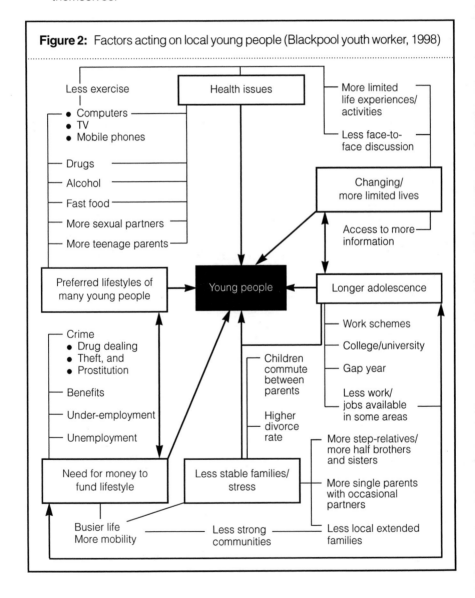

Figure 2: Factors acting on local young people (Blackpool youth worker, 1998)

When the diagram is explored, it becomes clear that **all** the factors in Figure 2 impact on the development of young people and their journey to independent adulthood. Each factor acts to either block or assist young people's development. One example of this is set out in the following case study.

Case Study: Sue and her mum. An example of the difficulties of young people gaining life experience.

Interviews with mother and daughter separately

Mother

When I was her age, we all used to play out on a piece of waste land. Lads and girls...we used to talk and drink, sometimes cider, and smoke fags too, talk about boys we fancied, planned weekends. We weren't angels. We used to play games a bit or watch the lads show off...We rowed too. Best friends split up and made up or moved on. It was great: no parents to hassle you...

...I don't let her play out much: there are needles all over and I don't think it's safe. She stays in or goes to her friends' houses or they come here...

I used to ride my bike all over the estate, but now it's too risky...so many cars speed and you never know who's about. Instead, I take her most places in the car. It's safer that way.

Sue (daughter)

Most evenings I'm in my room with Linda, Lisa and Di, or at theirs. We play CDs, talk and watch TV...We laugh a lot...talk about boys we fancy...We don't go out much. On Saturday, Mum takes me to swimming and on Tuesdays I go to the Majorettes. Sometimes it's a bit boring. When I'm 12 Mum is going to let me go into town on Saturday afternoon with Di. She'll pick us up from the bus station.   (Grange Park, Blackpool, 1999)

The issue here is one of community safety and this Case Study raises some questions:
- Where does Sue learn, and practice the social skills of:
  - making and keeping friends
  - disagreeing and staying friends
  - existing in groups outside the school environment?
- When does she begin to become independent: is being alone in town a big jump from total supervision?
- When and how does Sue begin to expand her very limited experience of life?

Twenty years ago, youth workers could assume that most young people would take the initial steps to independence naturally but this is no longer the case. The result is that youth workers need to develop programmes to ensure that young people take these first steps safely.

Sue and her mother's situation is just one example of how the changing world affects young people's experiences, and hence the work of the youth workers. The faster the social, political and economic situation of young people changes, the faster youth workers have to make responses.

A Broader Analysis

The following analysis, and see Figure 3, is taken from the National Youth Agency publication *Young People as Citizens Now* (1997), and is best read a section at a time. We recommend it to you but do not expect you to agree with it necessarily, but suggest that after each section, to test its correctness, you think about:

- your own experiences over the 20 years or so
- the young people you work with

The analysis suggests that there are seven factors which impact on young people. These factors add together and the result is that many young people do not receive:

> *...a preparation for life that is adequate or holistic. This results in young people...having a crisis of identity of meaning and purpose...About 20 per cent of young people react to this in risky ways...*

It is important to explore what these words mean. The headings are from *Young People as Citizens Now*. The discussion is our own.

Factors which impact on young people

1. Emotional development

Many young people come from unstable and incomplete families. Parents are often stressed and distressed. The effect of this can be to put young people's ability to develop relationships, or emotional attachments, at risk. Families can be affected by things beyond their control, for example:

- unemployment or risk of unemployment
- long-term illness of a family member
- other people's negative attitude to them
- absence of an extended family, e.g. grandparents, aunts
- loss of a family member, death, deportation, divorce
- the need for parents to work long hours
- repayments of loans, debts, mortgages and hire purchase

These are all factors that cause stress. Long-term stress can lead to people becoming unable to cope. The stress can lead to clinical depression and physical illnesses.

Think back to 1986 when young people you work with were born or very young. What was happening then for their parents?

Mrs Thatcher was Prime Minister. The miner's strike was recent. Coal, steel and shipbuilding industries had been privatised. Huge numbers of people were made redundant and the communities were decimated. The face of British industry had changed. Major factors affecting young people and their parents included:

- High unemployment leading to poverty and social discontent.
- Traditional work-based communities were breaking up. As the work places closed, traditions died and people moved away.
- Many people had houses with negative equity.
- One in three marriages ended in separation.

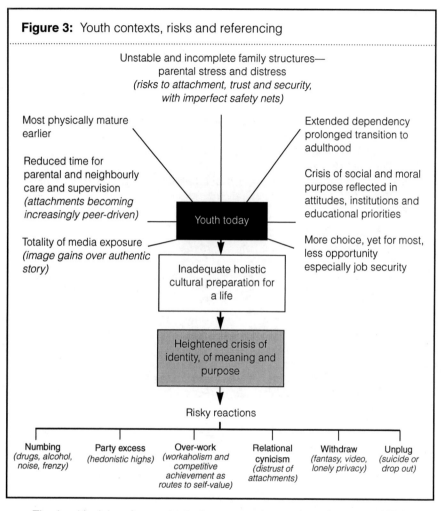

Figure 3: Youth contexts, risks and referencing

Unstable and incomplete family structures—
parental stress and distress
*(risks to attachment, trust and security,
with imperfect safety nets)*

Most physically mature
earlier

Reduced time for
parental and neighbourly
care and supervision
*(attachments becoming
increasingly peer-driven)*

Totality of media exposure
*(image gains over authentic
story)*

Extended dependency
prolonged transition to
adulthood

Crisis of social and moral
purpose reflected in
attitudes, institutions and
educational priorities

More choice, yet for most,
less opportunity
especially job security

Youth today

Inadequate holistic
cultural preparation for
a life

Heightened crisis of
identity, of meaning and
purpose

Risky reactions

Numbing	Party excess	Over-work	Relational cynicism	Withdraw	Unplug
(drugs, alcohol, noise, frenzy)	*(hedonistic highs)*	*(workaholism and competitive achievement as routes to self-value)*	*(distrust of attachments)*	*(fantasy, video, lonely privacy)*	*(suicide or drop out)*

- The health risks of unprotected sex were becoming clearer as AIDS was identified.
- Many parents were under stress for a variety of these and other reasons.

Many of the young people that you work with were born and grew up in this world. These societal changes had huge impact on individuals, families and their communities. It is a mistake to think of the effects only in terms of poverty. These changes devastated many people's lives; reduced opportunities and destroyed any sense of well being.

...they used us when they needed us; and abandoned us when they'd done.
(Former miner, South Wales, 1989)

Some young people have a completely different, but equally difficult, childhood. In an age of aggressive materialism, two wages are often seen as being necessary to ensure the payment of a mortgage and to have two cars and several holidays a year. Children can be materially well provided for, but lack attention from parents who struggle to cope with these pressures.

Case Study: Kev

Kev walked into the youth centre at 8.30 p.m. and began systematically smashing windows. He had never behaved in this way before. Mike, one of the workers, caught up with him and calmed him down.

This is Kev's story:

I'm fourteen today. When I came down for breakfast, everyone had gone. There was this envelope on the table. No card, not even my name on it. Dad had scribbled 'Happy Birthday son' on it. There was £150 in it. I tried to phone my Gran but she was out. I stayed off school in case she came round our house, but she never turned up. I had a drink this afternoon to celebrate nothing, but it made me sick so I came here to spend my f...birthday money. You know the rest.

Given the social circumstances described above, it is not surprising that many young people do not have the opportunities to learn to make and maintain effective relationships. This can:

- reduce their feelings of trust and security
- affect their emotional development
- affect the way they behave

In extreme cases, young people may become uncontrolled and uncontrollable. Emotional development begins with the ability to separate 'I feel' from 'I do'. For example, 'I feel embarrassed' therefore 'I respond by anger or by running away'. As we grow older we learn to separate the response from the feeling. This is called self control. We also learn how to put 'I feel' and 'I do' together in order to be creative and spontaneous. The ability to manage this process in a constructive way makes us emotionally mature or literate. 'Managing' the process by attention-seeking, bullying, tormenting people, withdrawal in its many forms and uncontrollable anger indicates emotional illiteracy.

2. Extended dependency and prolonged transition to adulthood

Without money you're no one: you can't do nowt. You've to wear crap clothes. It's dead embarrassing when your mates want to do things that cost and you've to drop out...I've to ask for money from me mam: she's not got nowt either.

(Young man 17, Doncaster, 2000)

In many ways, adulthood is related to economic independence. With money you can:

- Move away from home.
- Travel.
- Buy clothes and possessions that make you feel good.

- Be a part of the youth culture.
- Make choices about your life and be independent.
- Access higher education easily without a loan.

At the time of writing, the minimum wage is just under £4 per hour. A 40 hour week earns just over £150. For a young person living independently, once they have paid the basic costs for rent, food, services and so on, the amount of 'spending money' left for 'luxuries' is very small.

This may not be an attractive proposition to many young people. Given this situation, they may delay becoming independent for longer than previous generations did.

3. Young people become physically mature earlier

In 1960, adolescents reached sexual maturity between the ages of twelve and fourteen; now they do so between ten and twelve years. This, together with an increasingly open attitude to sex in the media, can place more pressure on young people to become sexually active at a younger age. This in itself carries risks of:

- Early pregnancy: for example, in parts of Doncaster, the rate of conception in fourteen-year-olds was 70 per 1000 young people (2000).
- Sexually transmitted diseases.
- Abusive relationships.

4. Reduced parental and neighbourly care and supervision

When communities were closer knit, each young person was known locally. This had the disadvantage of them often being 'labelled' but it did provide security, which in turn allowed them a measure of freedom. Further, the many eyes of the community ensured a measure of control. Young people did not, for the most part, have freedom without accountability to their community. The 1980s saw some major forces that challenged the existence of these communities and their ways of life.

Margaret Thatcher famously held the view that 'there is no such thing as society, only the individuals who compose them.' This set the scene for devaluing communities.

Changes in the industrial base resulted in the destruction of the communities who worked within them. Large areas of the country suffered, and continue to suffer, high levels of unemployment. More able people moved away to find work, leaving behind those who could not move, the old, the less qualified, carers and the sick.

5. The totality of media exposure

In the last 15 years there has been a revolution in the communications industry. Prices have fallen so that many young people have their own TV, CD player, video player, phone and computer with access to e-mail and the 'net'.

Young people's understandable enthusiasm for these items means that they are bombarded by images that bear very little relationship or relevance to their lives. However, they identify with the role models and life styles that are offered. They seek to become part of that life style by acquiring its trappings: designer clothes, fast foods, cars. The image becomes all consuming. Reality becomes 'boring'. The work required to have such a life style may be unattractive and unachievable.

Young people have, in theory, more choices than ever before. It is the age of the consumer. Great shopping malls are the new temples for consumers, who can:

- Purchase an incredible range of things via the Internet.
- Travel to most parts of the world.
- Live and work in different countries with relative ease.
- Have their faces and bodies remodelled should they desire.

However, in order to access these choices, people need:

- money
- confidence
- knowledge
- the skills to make appropriate choices

Many young people cannot access the choices, as they lack one or more of these essential ingredients. A relatively few young people do have access to a very wide range of alternatives and there is little limit on what they are able to do. These young people often work in the media, sports or IT industries and are role models for other young people. They set the standards for the desired lifestyle.

6. Crisis of social and moral purpose reflected in attitudes to institutional priorities

As they grow up, young people encounter many institutions, such as local authority schools, youth work provision and health services. These offer a humanistic set of values focused on:

- honesty, legality and conformity
- personal freedom
- equality of opportunity or anti-oppressive practice
- personal achievement
- team work
- material acquisition through achievement

However, these services tend to encourage young people to 'fit in' to society and become wage earning consumers. Little emphasis is placed on spirituality and morality. Young people who do not accept these values have few places where they can find alternatives. There are small pockets of culture that run counter to this. A few communities live by a common belief, outside of mainstream culture. These include some religious groups and those concerned with the peace movement, green issues, animal rights and volunteering.

How can young people find a belief system when they are faced with such a diversity of material choice and little opportunity to observe and explore the alternatives?

7. Young people are ill prepared for life

These factors combine to leave young people with a crisis of identity and with lives that lack meaning and purpose. They are ill prepared to face their futures.

> *They don't know where they're at, what they're doing or why they're doing it, so much of the time drifting like lost sheep...vulnerable. I know they don't look it, but they are, that's why they act so daft.*   (Youth worker, Liverpool)

The result of this is that some young people enter into 'risky reactions' (see Figure 3).

Chapter Two

Youth Work: Why We Need it More than Ever

Given the situation highlighted in Chapter 1, it is not surprising that young people are often perceived as a problem. As a group, young people are variously stereotyped, ignored, abused, judged, or condemned. They are blamed both for:

- Failing to conform to a world that was not of their making.
  They take drugs...respect no one...do as they please, they act as if it was their world.   (Wirral resident, 1999)

- Embracing the world they are born into too enthusiastically.
  They don't learn to cook, eat instant foods,...are only interested in material things, buy things because they are advertised...live on credit it's too easy to get.
                                                                    (The same resident)

They are seldom seen as vulnerable and in need of help. If you need evidence of this, read the papers, listen to politicians, watch TV and ask older adults how they feel about young people. Yet we can see from the analysis in Chapter 1, that many young people have been let down and made vulnerable by society.

Young people are seen as a threat. To counter this perceived threat, there is a limited range of responses:

- Education and empowerment.
- Welfare, based on the belief that some young people are deficient and this deficiency can be corrected by meeting their social, emotional and physical needs, so that they will fit into society.
- Pressure to conform: changes in the law to 'contain' young people, including changes to benefits.
- Punishment.
- Training to equip young people to find work in today's labour market and become conforming citizens.

Of these options, only **education** encourages young people to grow, and develop, and to take control of their own lives responsibly. Youth work is needed because only youth workers are educationalists, who focus on young people and advocate on their behalf.

1. Youth Workers Are Educationalists in a World Where Welfare and Training Dominate

Most agencies who work with young people, and most of the people in them, are more concerned with training, welfare, conformity and punishment, than with moving young people towards independent adulthood and autonomy:

- Schools, colleges, 'New Deal' and youth training are all concerned with training; they offer elements of education to varying degrees.
- Education welfare, social services and the health service are involved in welfare with elements of training and education.
- Probation, juvenile justice and Youth Offending Teams deal with welfare, training and punishment to various degrees.

All these agencies are promoting conformity.

2. Youth Workers' Focus is on Young People

Youth work is the only agency that is set up to offer learning, i.e. education in its broadest sense, to young people in a way that:

- Focuses on each young person as an individual.
- Works with young people based on relationships that are voluntary.
- Works with the whole young person, that is, their social, emotional, physical, spiritual and political development.
- Starts where young people are, not where we would like them to be.
- Tries to work non-judgementally.
- Treats young people as inexperienced adults by offering them respect as valued individuals.
- Seeks to give positive feedback and constructive criticism, and tries never to give negative feedback.
- Works through relationships built on trust, honesty, openness and caring.

It is concerned with listening to young people's thoughts, views and feelings because it is essential that young people have the opportunity to talk about and explore their ideas and to make sense of lives.

3. Youth Workers Advocate on Behalf of Young People and Help to Make their Voices Heard

Youth workers should work both to develop young people and advocate on their behalf. Other agencies all have important contributions to make to the growth and development of young people.

There is a developing trend for youth workers to work in other agencies: schools, juvenile justice, social services and multi-agency projects. Youth workers bring a special set of skills. They can relate to young people and win their trust and confidence. They can offer them learning in a way that young people can accept.

Sometimes the other agencies want these skills, but reject the value base of youth work. This puts workers in a difficult situation. It follows that it is vital for youth workers to learn to advocate:

- On behalf of youth work. Many people are unclear about the purpose of youth work, what it has to offer, how it conducts its work and its success. (See definition in introductory chapter.) Youth work needs its advocates now, perhaps more than at any point in the past.
- On behalf of young people and the situation in which they find themselves. and to help young peoples' voices to be heard.

This is the youth work response to the situation of young people.

Chapter Three

The Changed World of Youth Work

Once Upon a Time...

Up until the mid 1980s, youth work was unique in that it focused on delivering informal education to young people. It pioneered social, emotional and political education. During that time Local Authority Youth Services grew in size.

The youth service was seen as an 'add on'. There was no tradition of publicity or public relations in youth work. Very few people saw a need for it, they 'just got on with their work.' The youth service kept a low profile and workers commented that: 'No-one recognised the value of youth work'.

At that time, youth work tended to be a mixture of planned and unplanned work. Much of it was spontaneous. Record keeping and reporting tended to be minimal, and evaluation was often neglected. All the effort was put into working with young people, 'fun was high on the agenda for youth workers and young people alike'.

In the 1980s, that began to change.

Budgets became restricted

Youth work posts were cut, other economies were made. The result was that:

- Some posts remained unfilled, pending various reorganisations.
- Work loads increased.
- Some posts were lost and the duties were divided amongst other post holders.

There was a pattern of creating Area Worker posts to which full-time workers were appointed. The posts previously held by full-time workers were converted into part-time worker posts. The Area Workers managed a number of part-time workers in charge of clubs and projects. There was little training or support for these new arrangements. Part-time workers in charge often did not receive any training for their management role.

Services began to be reorganised so they had streamlined management structures. Support and supervision decreased. Training moved from a group-based approach to a portfolio-based one, thus restricting the element of group experience.

Young people became to be seen as more of a problem

Young people were seen as being more of a potential problem, as unemployment, poverty and crime all rose. There was genuine fear that these forces would de-stabilise society. Society wished to see young people constructively employed and more contained. This impacted on how funders saw the role of youth work.

The youth work curriculum was examined

Under the Thatcher government the school curriculum was redrawn. Ministers considered that it was logical to move on to review the learning offered by the only other major institution that worked with young people of thirteen and over, the youth service.

There was a national effort to define the youth work curriculum. Three ministerial conferences were held to draw this together, but no single definitive document was ever produced. Each local authority and voluntary agency went back to their own organisation to develop their own work. Youth work had been exposed as having no agreed and consistent written framework, although practice was fairly standard.

Increased public accountability

A move towards accountability in the spending of public money and of work undertaken by national and local government employees gathered momentum. Questions were asked of youth work:

- What was the purpose of youth work?
- What did youth workers do?
- How much did it cost to do it?
- How did these costs compare with other agencies?
- Were youth workers effective in reaching their targets, if they had set targets to reach?
- Was youth work good value for money?
- Where was the quality control in youth work?

This sent shock waves through the youth service as the questions proved difficult or impossible to answer. Youth workers felt that they were doing a good job, but did not always have a way of proving it. There was a lack of documentation.

Principal youth officers found themselves to be exposed, and responded by revising their policies, procedures and in some cases reorganising their service yet again! The result was a rash of new:

- policy statements
- mission statements
- quality indicators and targets
- forms

The last of these was to ensure that youth workers planned and evaluated their work through:

- annual and termly plans
- annual and termly reports
- nightly and weekly returns

The volume of administration increased.

Health and safety requirements became tighter

There was a series of high profile accidents, involving young people, including:

- Cairngorms disaster
- Land's End tragedy
- Austrian field trip tragedy
- Lyme Bay canoeing tragedy

Each tragedy caused Local Authorities and other organisations to tighten up, revisit or rewrite their procedures. National legislation (AALA) was introduced which inspected outdoor education centres and their employers, who were often local education authorities. It caused many to rework their policies and procedures. Organisations started to insist on staff having specific nationally recognised qualifications for taking young people out on trips. These qualifications were over and above their youth work or teaching certificates.

Legislation in the 1980s demanded that any situation with a potential for harm to individuals had to be risk-assessed formally. Youth workers found themselves having to prove and formally record, that a huge range of activities are safe and properly managed. Previously some of these activities had been carried out spontaneously.

Now everyone who works with young people is required to show that the activities:

- Are appropriate to the young people involved.
- Are led by suitably qualified and experienced people.
- Take place in the appropriate environment with the correct equipment.

Risk assessments are required in order to demonstrate that the leader of the activity has taken all the safety factors into consideration. Additionally, there is much more emphasis on showing that activities have been thoroughly planned.

In large organisations there are manuals that set out safety requirements, and procedures for huge ranges of activities, from archery through cooking to woodwork and yachting.

Many individuals expect to sue if something goes wrong. There is much less acceptance of risk as a part of day-to-day life. 'Where there is blame, there will be a claim.' It has now become essential that youth workers ensure the safety of the young people in any activity they undertake. They must also record the process in a way that will stand up in court.

No price can be put on safety, but the effect of these changes is to cause another increase in the workload. It makes it much harder for youth workers to be able to respond spontaneously.

Child protection

Following the revelation of a large number of incidents of child abuse in, for example, residential care homes, procedures have been changed to increase young people's safety. Legal requirements mean that all those who work with young people must be vetted by police and trained in child protection procedures and practices. This is necessary, but takes time and is a further pressure on youth workers. It can result in long delays in newly appointed staff taking up a post as they await their police clearance.

And The Result...

The result of these changes is that the culture of youth work has changed. Youth work is no longer so spontaneous; planning is an absolute requirement, as is the paperwork that goes with it. Youth work is under scrutiny, and in the public view, more than ever before.

But what does this mean in reality?

Case Study: Ahmed

It was 10 p.m. The young people had only just left the centre and the staff team had had a short meeting about the session. Issues included:

- Who would work with Pat (aged 14): she needed extra support and her behaviour was difficult to manage?
- What should they do about the 'tackling racism' project: how much more work was needed?
- How were they going to manage to cover for staffing shortages next week?

Ahmed, the worker in charge looked tired. He checked the money, completed the nightly report sheet and then stuffed the pay claims into his bag to do at home. He then reached across and picked up a pile of papers and flicked through them.

I need to read them: they're important. I don't know when, though. Look at them all:
The Youth Forum application and details: I need to reply to that.
Format for the Annual Report: deadline last week.
*Stuff on the **Connexions** meeting I'm supposed to go to.*
Loads of internal bulletins and memos.
I only work fifteen hours and twelve of them are face-to-face, and that only leaves me three to keep the project going: when am I supposed to do all this?

He stared at the pile and then a smile lit up his face:

Kev's on the list for the Youth Forum: six months ago he'd have told us to 'f... off' if we'd have suggested it.

Ahmed's situation is no different from that of thousands of other part- and full-time workers. We are all working so hard at delivering our job that we rarely make enough time to read or think. This traps us in the here and now. We cope with crises as they hit us. We never have enough time or space to plan new work and manage our time better. We tend not to see the wider picture. We are responsive rather than pro-active.

It is difficult to develop strategies and plans without understanding the wider picture, and how all its parts relate to one another. Yet planning and working systematically is the only way we can become more effective and less stressed as workers. This is why we need to change the way we work and manage our boundaries and time more effectively even when it means saying 'no'. It is one of the ways that we prevent being 'kippered'.

And the Positive Side?

On a positive note, the result of these changes is that there are more opportunities for youth workers to:
- Tell the wider public about the situation of young people.
- Promote the work that they are doing and the advantages of the 'youth work way of doing things'.

The regulations help to ensure that:
- The standard of youth work is more consistent.
- Young people receive a high quality service.
- Young people are generally safer in the care of youth workers.

The youth workers are at a crossroads. They have a choice; either to:
- Complain about the extra rules and regulations.
- Comply with them, but reluctantly.
- Do as little as possible in these areas.
- Keep a low profile and hope the issues never affect them.

Or they can:
- Make the system work for them.
- Use the issues to raise the status of youth work.
- Campaign on behalf of, and with, young people.
- Fight for a larger, better resourced service.
- Argue for paid training to ensure that all youth workers, whether part-time, full-time or voluntary, are resourced to carry out their work.
- Press for managers who understand the difficulties of delivering quality youth work today.
- Press for managers to be trained to supervise and support youth workers to achieve this.

As a service, if youth workers take the first road they will cease to exist. Youth work will simply be incorporated into other agencies. Its uniqueness will be lost and 'youth work' will cease to empower young people. In the words of one principal officer:

> The workers groan under the paperwork. They say that they are drowning in it and that they came into the service to work with young people. I understand how they feel, but we can't put the clock back...We have no option, the culture has changed and we all have to get on with it or go under.

As workers, if we take the first road of complaining then we will remain 'kippered'. If we take the second approach we can begin to 'unkipper' ourselves. This requires us to:
- Be pro-active as opposed to re-active.
- Control our work positively.
- Publicise the value of youth work and its way of delivering learning to young people.

Policy makers, managers, parents and the wider community all need to be aware of this message if we are to succeed.

Chapter Four

Defining Good Youth Work

There is a story that may or may not have its origins in truth:

> *Matt had been going to the local youth centre for six months. His mother decided that she ought to go and see what they did there. She called at about 8.30 p.m. It was a busy night. Two young people welcomed her and took her to see George, the full-time worker in charge. She explained why she had come and George asked two young people to show her around. They took her through the coffee bar where a group was planning a visit to Hungary. They pointed out the murals done by members over a number of years. She saw the arts and craft room where the women's group were working on entertainment for a local hospital. In the yard she saw where the young men and women had set out an outdoor training circuit. She returned via the counselling room: she couldn't enter of course, but her guides explained to her about the help-line that the youth council had established. The young people returned her to George who was in the office talking to a young woman about her portfolio for her Youth Achievement Award. The mother's comment was 'What an interesting hobby you have George but what's your real job?'*

Obviously the joke has its origins in the fact that few people actually know what youth workers do and youth workers are bad at explaining this. If you asked people what youth workers do the general view is often that:

- A 'youth worker is a type of social worker who gets on well with young people.'
- 'They keep them out of trouble by doing things with them and often work with difficult young people whom no-one else wants to know.'
- 'Some do it voluntarily, like guides and scouts. A few are paid, but why that is, people are unsure. They do a bit of training to make sure they do things safely.'

In most groups of adults, there are those who have had experiences of youth clubs, projects or voluntary organisations. They tend to speak warmly of the youth workers and say how a youth worker helped them and were good to them, but they seldom specify what the youth worker actually did.

When asked to describe their job, youth workers often rely on words and phrases that mean little to the general public:

> *We work to empower young people; to help them take control of their lives.*
> *Youth workers build relationships with young people...and help them to become effective adults.*
> *We offer them learning opportunities through which they grow and develop.*
> *We help young people do what they want to do.*

Alternatively, youth workers offer a long explanation:

Well, it's hard to explain in a sentence, can I give you an example? We were working with Mike (that's not his real name, I can't tell you that because of confidentiality, you might recognise him from what I say). Mike had this problem...

No wonder workers can sometimes be seen as being woolly minded! There are a number of difficulties in describing youth work.

Identifying the skills

The first problem is that although the delivery of youth work is very highly skilled, youth workers are not always aware of the skills they are using. When they can describe their skills, they can accurately communicate what they are doing. Then, instead of saying things like:

Well, I just do it: I don't really know why it works, it just does.

They would be able to say:

I begin by making young people feel safe, no one can learn if they don't feel safe. I make opportunities for young people to talk to me about things that matter to them: for them to tell me their story. If a young person is a bit shy, I always try to...etc.

When people understand what youth workers do, and why they do it, they tend to be more sympathetic and supportive. It can also help people to be more aware of the difficulties that young people face.

All adults are potential voters, so they can influence how youth work is funded. Youth work and young people need the public's understanding and support.

Define what youth work is for you, and enrich your definition by giving examples and illustrations from the place that you work.

The wide range of youth work

The second difficulty about offering an explanation is that youth work takes place in a very wide range of settings using a diverse set of activities. These include:

- Detached or outreach work and work in mobile centres.
- Clubs that may operate every night of the week in large urban centres, or once a week in rural areas.
- Specific project work, for example, the Duke of Edinburgh's Award, youth theatres, adventure clubs.
- Work in units based on the identity of the young people (young women's groups, groups of black young people, PHAB groups, groups for young people who are lesbian, gay or bisexual).
- In specialist projects based around such issues as health, prostitution.
- There are information services, one stop information shops and centres that offer counselling.

Youth workers may work in a wide range of other settings: colleges, schools, health centres, social service units as well as in multi-agency projects such as Connexions, Youth Offending Teams and social inclusion units.

This is a complex situation, difficult to explain to people quickly. It can be put like this:

> *Youth workers work wherever young people are: in clubs, on the streets, in schools. The work is the same, it just takes place in a range of settings.*

Competition between different settings for youth work

Some workers often see the work in their setting as being more relevant and appropriate than work in another setting. For example, workers say:

> *Detached work is where its at. We work with young people on their territory. This gives them power...they don't see us as an institution like building-based work.*

> *I work in a youth club, everyone says we are irrelevant and old-fashioned but where else is work so embedded in the community? The workers are off the estate: many were members themselves. Young people hear about the club from their parents, we're part of their scene...each generation makes the club their own.*

> *The Duke of Edinburgh's Award is fantastic. OK, so we do appeal to lots of kids who achieve more, they've got needs too, but we also run groups aimed at including disaffected young people. Our young people get a tremendous sense of achievement; a nationally recognised qualification...*

There is a need for youth workers to celebrate that they work in a range of different ways. This level of differentiation means that a wide range of young people have their needs met. Additionally, they can move on to different things as their needs change. Youth workers offer a highly accessible and differentiated service. Working in different ways requires different skills. Youth workers are multi-talented.

Why working with the individual is important

We need to tell people that youth workers are not specialists, they are the last of the generalists and they should be proud of this. Educational establishments such as schools, colleges and universities offer a fixed curriculum and a system that takes the learners through it. Youth work is different, youth work starts where young people are, not from where we would like them to be. We identify their learning needs and design a learning pathway through which individuals and groups can have their needs met. It follows that because the learning pathway is based on the age, experience, needs and interests of individuals and groups of young people, the activities that make up the pathway are very wide-ranging.

In summary:

> *Schools and colleges work on fixed programmes of learning. Youth workers are different: they base their work on the young people's needs and interests.*
> *We use this as a starting point to offer young people learning that is relevant to their lives and appropriate to their age, experience and interest.*
> *We offer a tailor made service of individual learning pathways.*

Why making a relationship is paramount

Finally, youth workers are justifiably proud of offering learning through the caring, equal, relationships that they make with young people. People often do not understand how important this is. From their point of view:

> *Why do you need a relationship to do what you do? Why don't you just get on with it and set things up for them?*

When people say this, we need to explain that many young people do not have good experiences of adult relationships. It is important that they develop a good relationship with someone, to help them to become skilled parents, or good working colleagues, or friends. Youth workers act as role models so young people can learn and develop skills such as:

- caring and being cared for
- disagreeing and remaining friends
- negotiation and compromise
- building relationships that are open, honest and based in trust

The skills of describing our work to others in ways that they can understand and sympathise with are vital. These descriptions, however, must not betray the work. This is the platform from which we can obtain wide support for the work.

Chapter Five

Identifying and Meeting Young People's Needs

This is a systematic process underpinned by several theories. However, before considering the theory, here are three examples of work that is:

- needs led
- systematically planned
- evaluated

All are based on the NAOMIE framework explained below.

Identifying and Meeting the Needs

Once the needs are known, the worker has to decide how to work systematically to meet the needs. One approach is to use the **NAOMIE** model:

N Identifies the **Needs**.

A Set the **Aim**: whatever it is that you are working towards.

O Set the **Objectives**: those smaller steps that will get you to your aim.

M Decide what **Method** you are going to use.

I Decide what **Indicators** you will use to show you are on course, then go ahead and **Implement** it.

E Decide how you are going to **Evaluate** the outcomes and review the process.

Each of these Case Study examples occurred in a different context.

El's involved a neighbourhood worker on an estate and took place over ten weeks. Niek's occurred in an information shop and was completed in two hours. Peta's concerned the development of one person over three years using the Duke of Edinburgh's Award. What these cases have in common is that they:

- Began with needs identification.
- Involved systematic planning to meet the needs of young people, to evaluate, review and feedback to them.

Such work is at the heart of good practice when working with young people.

Case Study: El

Needs

El is a 16-year-old young woman who lives with her mother and two younger brothers on a run down nearby estate. She is intelligent and doing well at school. She is a confident and able athlete but the school has no capacity to develop this. She hangs out with three friends in her class: Chevella, Kay and Leanne, they have been friends since year five at junior school. El is the leader of the group, the ideas person, she takes the lead in finding fun things to do. She tells you that she is bored as there is nothing to do on the estate and she has no money to get off it. She wants to go to college if she can and has a cousin who is a lawyer: she likes the sound of that. She and her friends are beginning to get into difficulties. They steal from the local shop and smoke cannabis. Her mother came to see the worker, she is very concerned about what is happening. El spends a lot of her time looking after her two younger brothers (aged 8 and 6) during the school holidays as her mum works until 5.30 p.m. The mum seems tired, stressed and in need of support.

Identification of Needs
The Neighbourhood worker felt that:

1. El is lacking stimulation and challenge. She wants and needs achievement.
2. In some ways she is a young adult too soon because of her 'parenting' role in relationship to her brothers. Her growth is stunted socially, emotionally, spiritually and politically because of the lack of opportunities locally.

This is resulting in her finding challenge, stimulation and fun in ways that are not positive and are illegal. This is discussed with El and she spontaneously agrees that this is the case.

Aim
To provide El with learning opportunities to help her reach her potential.

Objectives
To offer El new experiences with which she can continue away from the estate.
To keep her and her friendship group together in the process.
To support El in the leadership role that she has begun to develop.
To support her mother in her parenting of El and her two brothers.

Method
The worker has a link with social services and they have a small amount of money to be used for taking young people on holiday who would not otherwise have had that opportunity. Simply providing a holiday would only meet the first two objectives. Instead the worker decided to run a short programme:
Stage 1. Ask the four young women if they would like to help run a holiday for ten young people who would otherwise not have had a holiday. This would involve some fund raising off the estate.
Stage 2. Fund raise: letters, phone calls and visits.
Stage 3. Plan the holiday. This will include visiting the holiday venue and trying out the activities. The idea is that the young women will enjoy themselves and learn about the organisation and safety.
Stage 4. Run a planning weekend.
Stage 5. Run the holiday with the young people: these will include El's two brothers. This will give the mother a break and it may be possible to get the brothers involved in an after-school club and a play scheme in the future.

The periods between each stage are used to look at the young women's:
- achievements

- roles, including leadership
- support mechanisms
- and to offer positive feedback and constructive criticism

Stage 6. After the programme: the group was asked if they would like to join the town's volunteer programme, which has Millennium Volunteers funding and can pay expenses. Volunteers go away from the area most weekends.

Indicators

Do the young women want to join in?
Do they turn up for the slog of fund-raising?
Do they remain involved?
How do they respond to leaving the estate and meeting new people?
What roles do they take up?
How is El working as a leader in all of this?
Is the young people's participation real or are they just hanging in there for the sake of the holiday?
Can they identify their learning?
Do they turn up for the planning weekend: are they active participants?
Do they turn up for the holiday, do they stay in role as helpers or do they behave like big children?

Evaluation
Formative evaluation

After each session, and the planning weekend, the following questions need exploring to discover how each young person is developing:

- What has happened that is of significance to the young people's learning?
- What needs to be done to progress their learning?
- The programme's successes?
- Its not so successful parts?
- What role did you take?
- What have we all learned?

Summary evaluation (at the end)

- What did the children get from the holiday?
- Did it go to plan?
- Good bits, bad bits, points to look out for if done again?
- What has each of us achieved and learned?

For the record, the project ran to the end. All the children had a holiday that they would not forget for a long time. El became totally absorbed in the project and grew in confidence and skills through the whole process. Her friends were not so enthusiastic: they enjoyed the weekend and the holiday, but found the fund-raising and planning 'a bit boring'.

Each gained and developed in a number of ways. Only El went on to join the volunteers groups and goes away with them most weekends. She still spends weekdays and evenings with her friends. Just recently, she came to see the youth worker. She asked why they did not fight to get more resources on the estate, instead of working to expand people's worlds by leaving it.

Case Study: Niek

The planning and delivery may only take one or two hours.

Needs

Niek is 19, a quiet, tall young man. He lives with his family (mother, father, grandmother, and two older siblings) on the estate. He has a long-standing girlfriend and they intend to get a flat together when they can afford it. Niek plays the drums in a group formed from friends he met doing his A-levels at the local sixth form college. He seldom goes off the estate. He has applied for a course at University to do computer studies and is due to go for the interview next week. The University is far enough away from home for him to have to live there in term time.

He has sought out the local information service explaining that he is not going for the interview. He cannot explain why, except to say, 'it isn't here: all my life is here'. He is obviously distressed.

Aim

To help Niek to make a considered decision about his future.

Objectives

To help Niek to:

- Identify what his reasons are for not wanting to go to the interview.
- Identify the range of possibilities that exist, for example:
  - dealing with the issues of going to the interview
  - doing a computer course elsewhere
  - considering other possibilities for his future
  - making decisions about the interviews and perhaps about his future.

Method

Niek is an analytical thinker: that is why he is so good with computers. He is not so good at talking about feelings. He finds eye contact quite difficult.

The method chosen was to stick four pieces of flip chart paper on the wall, provide coloured pens and to support and encourage Niek to work through the process of analysing his situation. Niek was asked to list all the things that were going through his mind about his future. He was then able to group these factors and make links between the groups. Niek used this analysis to answer the questions that he was posing himself.

Indicators

- Can Niek get into this method?
- Does it engage him?

It was necessary to have alternative methods in mind as time was short and this method does not suit everyone. Alternatives included:

1. Working with Niek and his girlfriend.

2. Directing him to the careers service.

3. Making contact with the access section of the University to see if they can help.

Evaluation

Niek took to the methodology like a duck to water. He remarked, 'I never thought it would be so easy to sort things out like this'.

After about an hour he decided to:

- Go to the interview for practice.
- Take up the worker's offer of having a practice interview before going to the interview.
- Explore the possibility of getting a job locally and doing a degree with the Open University or by a distance learning package.

He recognised his difficulties in leaving the area and in talking about feelings, but did not feel like facing these at this time. He was offered a place at the University and was extremely proud of this but didn't take it up. He did a distance learning course that he completed satisfactorily and was supported in the process through a job.

It is not always practical or necessary to design a piece of work to meet a specific young person's or group's needs. The programme that the unit is running can be a vehicle for this.

Case Study: Peta

This is a summary of some 50 cycles through the NAOMIE process over three years.

Peta was 16 and had had a very difficult life. She had been abused by one of her mother's boyfriends. At 14 she was a prostitute and using alcohol and drugs in dangerous quantities. She was very aggressive, had low self esteem and self harmed on a regular basis. She had few skills in making relationships and was very lonely.

After a referral, a Duke of Edinburgh's Award worker formed a relationship with her, as a means of working with her.

In the next two and a half years, Peta made two unsuccessful suicide attempts and spent six weeks in hospital, as her mother had rejected her and she refused to go anywhere else. She also spent nine weeks in an adolescent unit. She walked out, despite the fact that she was doing well. She assaulted two young people and an Award worker, and returned to prostitution and drugs, on various occasions.

The Award scheme worker did not give up on Peta, and little by little she completed sections of the Award. These were tangible measures of her personal growth and development. She became less aggressive and more consistent. Each completed section raised her self esteem and confidence, although Peta herself would not admit this.

The major difficulty was the expedition section that required Peta to work with three others for two days in the countryside. No other young people wanted to work with her as she was disruptive. Peta sensed this and did not want to be with them. At the third attempt, she managed to complete the practice and final expedition with the same group. She recognised this as the massive move forward that it was. The mixture of systematic working through cycles of NAOMIE together with:

- befriending
- modelling
- instructing
- and never giving up

- counselling
- coaching
- doing things together

…began to move her on. She still has a long way to go but is thinking about her Silver Award.

Chapter Six

How People Learn

The role of the youth worker is to meet young people's needs by offering them **learning experiences** that are:

- fun
- appropriate to their age, background, skills and experience
- relevant to their development

To do these things, youth workers must understand how people learn, and then build the theory into their practice.

Some Key Points About How People Learn

1. Building and maintaining a safe learning climate

It is very hard to learn if you feel unsafe. Think back to your own experiences of learning and list things that made you feel safe, or unsafe. Each individual would make their own list, but might include the following:

Safe	Unsafe
Being with friends	Feeling alone
A friendly tutor or teacher	Demanding or unapproachable tutor or teacher
Calm atmosphere	Boisterous, noisy atmosphere
Small groups	Large groups
Starts at a point you can understand	Starts beyond your comprehension
Right speed, not too fast	Too fast to follow
Physically comfortable environment	Uncomfortable environment, too hot or cold, chairs too hard, too far away
Receiving praise for success	Being (or fear of) put down or derided
Tutor uses accessible language	Tutor uses technical terms or jargon
No physical or emotional threats	Feeling threatened or emotionally at risk
Understanding what learning is being offered and what the learner is expected to achieve	The learner having previously failed at what they are trying to learn

A friendly atmosphere is one where there are many 'put-ups' and few 'put-downs.' Put-ups motivate people and make them feel good: put-downs de-motivate people and make them feel bad. Motivated people learn more easily.

Put-ups	Put-downs
Smiles, responding to people	Autocratic, bossy manner
Remembering names and what has happened previously	Treating people as statistics, not as people
Offering praise	Being disparaging
Laughing **with** people	Laughing **at** people
Acknowledging achievement and effort	Harping back to previous failures
Being supportive	Being discouraging
Treating people as equals	Treating people with contempt

The list refers to relatively small pieces of behaviour. Put ups make people feel valued and included. Put downs devalue and exclude. Of course, those workers who are put down will not work to their full potential. You do not need to read widely or go on long courses to get this right. All you need to do is:

- Be aware of how you behave towards others.
- Ask yourself the question, 'how would I feel if I was treated the way I am treating others?'
- Ask the people you manage what they find helpful about your style and what they find unhelpful.
- If you get it wrong, accept responsibility, apologise and try to put it right. Most people do not hold a grudge if someone genuinely tries to put things right.

If you do these things it will show you are human and that is a good place to start, it creates a safe learning climate.

You can also ask those you work with to make their own list of what makes them feel **safe** or **unsafe**. When the list is complete, ask people to try acting in a way that makes people feel safe. Review the list, and people's agreement to it, occasionally, or whenever someone feels the contract is not being kept. The list is not law, change it to make it work for you and those you work with. Ask the young people:

- What makes it safe, and unsafe, for them to learn?
- How does the environment feel here?

The only potential problem with building a safe learning climate is that it can make life too cosy. People may lack challenge and debate, resulting in:

- a lack of creativity
- people being afraid of trying new things
- feeling unsafe in the outside world

So, all youth workers must try to hold and maintain a safe learning climate at all times in working with young people.

2. Giving feedback

It is possible to learn without realising it. Feedback and review help people to recognise what they have learned, and to value the learning. The simplest form of feedback is **positive feedback**, or praise, from the worker or tutor:

Well done
You tried hard

Did you think that you could do that?
It was good that you...

This motivates and encourages people. Many young people receive very little praise in their lives. Praise them wherever you can, but never give false praise, which will be recognised for what it is: dishonest and worthless. If possible, be precise about the young person's achievement:

Well done: you all listened to each other before you began to plan.
Great, Jo usually leads the group and she couldn't come. Wes and Sion filled the gap excellently.

Giving specific feedback helps young people to repeat their achievements, and to identify and value their learning. Beware though, of **negative** rather than **positive feedback**, that is, blame rather than praise. Our culture often seems to focus on blame. Remarks such as:

You're hopeless at that
What a load of rubbish?

serve only to reduce confidence and self-esteem. Instead, ask the young people to tell you something they have recently done, of which they are proud.

In addition, encourage young people to **give each other** positive feedback. They often have little or no experience of giving this sort of feedback and may find it embarrassing unless they practice. Teaching young people how to praise each other, means that they are learning to encourage the development of others, a skill that is essential to building adult relationships, and particularly, to being a parent.

3. The Gothenburg School of Learning

This is a very brief summary of the Gothenburg principles of learning. Imagine that this rectangle in Figure 4a is a picture of everything that is known about car engines and if you could get inside my head, you could plot a graph, like this, of what I know.

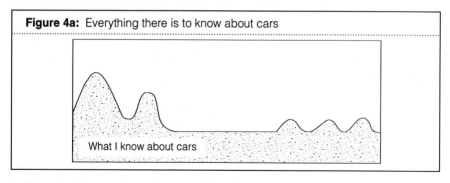

Figure 4a: Everything there is to know about cars

What I know about cars

If you had to teach me about engines you might start by saying:

In order to understand the change of pressure within the piston chamber...

The learning you are offering is so far from what I know that I cannot understand it and I would think:

What a clever instructor: but I can't follow it at all.

Figure 4b shows what would happen.

Figure 4b: Learning so far removed from my knowledge that I cannot understand or retain it

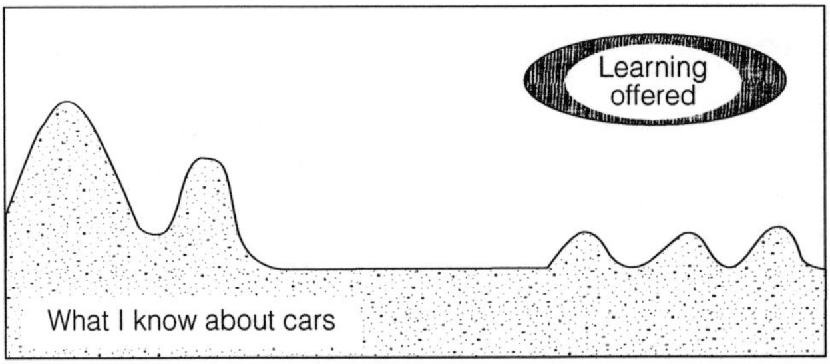

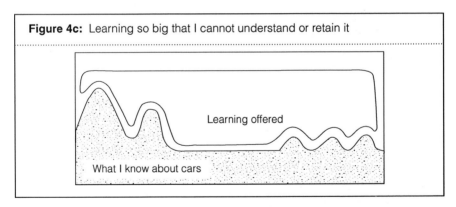

If you could match the learning that you offered with what I know, as in Figure 4c, I would say:

I understand every word: but it was too much I've got mental indigestion and I can't remember it.

Figure 4c: Learning so big that I cannot understand or retain it

But if you offered me a right-sized, bite-sized piece of learning, as in Figure 4d, I could absorb it and in a few minutes I wouldn't even remember that you taught me. It would feel as if I always knew it.:

But beware, I may need some 'unlearning,' I might feel:

I'm hopeless at practical things, I always get it wrong, and get wound up...

or

People like me don't know about car engines.

In either case, I would need to unlearn, that is, to change my view of myself, my self image, before I could move on to learn about car engines, see Figure 4e.

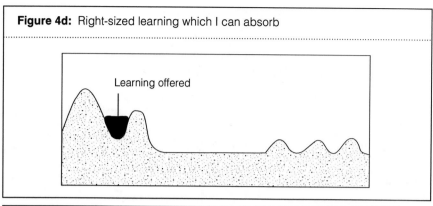

Figure 4d: Right-sized learning which I can absorb

Learning offered

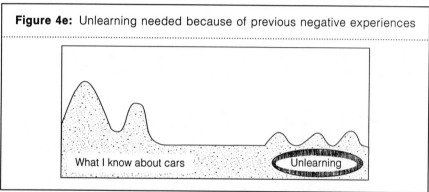

Figure 4e: Unlearning needed because of previous negative experiences

What I know about cars

Unlearning

Unlearning is harder than learning especially if it is about a part of your self image. The only way to change is to give young people smaller experiences, where each piece is successful. This way they grow in confidence and the experience of success causes them to change how they see themselves. Any failure along the way will confirm their self image and a great deal of the 'unlearning' will be lost. People around them must give them the space to change and confirm their achievements.

Remember that, in general, people learn more by doing things than by reading about them, being told about them or watching them. Guided experience is a powerful learning method.

Some people learn easiest by understanding a little piece at a time and building up to the bigger picture. Others do it the other way round. They need the whole picture before they can begin to focus on a part.

Many people have blocks to learning. These could include poor hearing or eyesight, language difficulties, dyslexia or a bad experience. Part of the skill of offering learning opportunities is to look out for any blocks and to work with the individual to find a way round these difficulties.

Chapter Seven

Identifying Young People's Needs

Read this chapter with Chapters 4 and 5: all these chapters are linked together.

Needs and Wants: The Difference...

At its simplest, **needs** are things that we must have in order to live and thrive:
- water, food, warmth, shelter, clothes
- friends, security, challenge, stimulation
- liking yourself

Wants are the things that we would like to have, but can live without, if necessary:
- large amounts of money
- holidays abroad
- digital TV
- fashion clothes
- a new car
- public recognition and fame

Wants are often material things. Ask young people to identify what they see as needs and wants. Their analysis may go something like this:

Needs	Wants
to be treated like an adult to have friends not to be bored/have fun to go on away days/holidays help with English/Maths to get alcohol legally for pot to be legalised good clothes money	money new trainers mobile phone car/motor bike own room to be a star sex

Their definitions blur the boundaries of the simple definitions.

Case Study: Tom

Tom's friends all have designer clothes and refuse to go round town with him, because his mum gets his clothes from the market, are those designer clothes Tom's wants or needs?

Mum sees them as a want:

We can't afford all that...I have enough trouble putting food on the table... anyway you destroy your clothes in a week.

From Tom's perspective:
If I don't get the right threads, I've no mates. She doesn't understand...everyone will call me...I won't be able to go out ever.

Separating needs from wants means knowing each individual young person well. This is the first step in identification of needs.

Identification of Needs: The Theory

Most youth workers are good at identifying needs but often find it difficult to explain the mechanisms by which they do it. It is important to learn to do this in order to:
- Help inexperienced youth workers to develop these skills.
- Explain to other professionals and parents the basis of our work.

Three researchers in particular (Maslow, Button and Pringle) have produced work that gives us insight into the needs of young people.

1. Maslow's hierarchy of needs

Maslow suggests that it is not possible to move towards meeting the higher needs if the basic needs are not met. For example, in the absence of food, warmth and safety, no one is able to focus on meeting other needs. This could be for no other reason than that their time and energy is used up fighting for sheer survival.

2. Button and Pringle's theory

Button and Pringle's work can be combined, to provide a framework of emotional requirements for use in identifying young people's needs:

Need of friendship

Friends, mates, a family group, people who offer unconditional love and affection. People around you who make you feel valuable and of value, who give you positive feedback and constructive criticism.
People who are there for you and want you to succeed.

Need of security

Knowing that there will always be food, warmth and somewhere to live. Being free of the fear of physical violence, emotional attacks, bullying, rejection and scapegoating. Never having to accept responsibilities that are more rightly those of an older adult, such as bringing up a family, being the major carer of a family, or the wage earner.

Need of stimulation

Doing exciting things that break the pattern of everyday life. Doing activities that are creative, experiencing a range of emotions in a safe environment. Examples of stimulating activities include dancing, drama and sport, art work, playing with children, looking after animals.

Need of challenge

Trying something that you do not know that you can do, conquering your fear, enjoying success, coping with failure and learning from it and perhaps having another go. Transferring experience in one activity to another. Developing mental strength and tenacity. Supporting others when you feel you need support yourself.

Need to cope with authority

Coping with people who have power, e.g. the police, teachers, parents, and officials, in an assertive, adult way. Learning to handle personal power in a positive way. This is a preparation for adult life, and for being a parent.

Need to cope with sexuality

Accepting of self as a sexual being with the responsibility to self and others that this entails. Accepting others as sexual beings and that there are a range of different expressions of this. Understanding that sexual relationships are about equality and enjoyment, never about oppression, or exploitation, in unequal power relationships.

Need to develop a positive view of self

Feeling OK as a person and that so are others, who may be different but this makes life richer and more interesting. Having no need to force others to be like you. Knowing what you are good at, what you are not good at and what you want to improve. Being able to learn from experiences and to accept criticism. Being able to recognise when you have made a mistake and deal with it. Being assertive.

3. *Young people's developmental needs*

Young people need to develop in the following areas; each description is only intended to give a flavour of what each area contains:

Emotionally

Being able to describe and discuss feelings, and recognising that others have feelings and respond to these appropriately.

Socially

The ability to:
- build and maintain relationships with a wide range of people
- communicate accurately
- treat people as equal and valuable
- read situations
- cope in a wide range of situations

Physically

Developing the skills of balance and co-ordination as well as speed and stamina. Having body knowledge and confidence. Building a strong body and enjoying physical activity. Understanding how your body works and what it needs to keep fit and well.

Cognitively

Being able to use the full range of thinking skills, that is, defining, comparing, contrasting, using a matrix, analysing, synthesising, and thinking creatively.

Spiritually

Developing a sense of right and wrong, an ethical base for life with a value base that helps decision making. Working out how you believe the world should be and having a sense of wonder at what it contains. Understanding the wide range of beliefs that exist about deities and spirituality, and respecting others' beliefs. Understanding and developing your own beliefs about gods, the soul and the spirit.

Academically

To be able to read and write and use information technology. To be able to learn from your experiences, to think independently and to work out your own learning pathway for something that interests you. It may include knowing about the history and geography of the world and how it affects us today. Understanding the inter-relationship of living things. Learning practical skills, languages, literature and much more.

Politically

Understanding power and how it works. Being able to use your own power well and to be able to understand and interact with the systems that control our lives. Voting in local and national elections, using complaints' procedures effectively. Coping with the legal system. Make decisions about joining unions, understanding that politics is a part of all aspects of everyday life. Taking a position on Green issues, health, work, and financial matters.

Empowerment

Young people need to be able to make decisions about who they want to be and how they want to live their life. Careers' decisions, work, financial matters, job seeking and holding skills. All aspects of independent living. Also to be able to make their views known in a way that effects change.

These frameworks, Maslow's hierarchy of needs, Button and Pringle's combined work, and the theory of areas of development, all offer youth workers a theoretical understanding of what an individual young person needs to become an effective adult.

The youth workers' job is to use these frameworks to:
- Identify where a young person is in all these areas.
- Work out which pieces of learning are the most significant to the young person's learning at present.

This is where the skills of youth work come in.

Your Skills of Identification: The Practice

There are four ways of identifying a young person's needs:

1. Observation.
2. Listening.
3. Activities.
4. Investigation.

1. Observing them non-judgementally

This is difficult, as it is so easy to be judgemental. For instance, think about the difference between the statements:

- The young woman was in dirty jeans.
- The young woman was in paint-stained but freshly-washed jeans.
- The young woman was in jeans that she had worn all day at work. They were splattered with paint.

The first statement is judgemental. Dirty implies a lack of attention to personal cleanliness. The other statements are more precise and objective. Now consider the following statement:

> The young woman approached the chip shop angrily. She stopped and spoke to two small girls. One gave her some money. She went in and bought some chips which she sat and ate without offering the little girls any.

The implication here is that a nasty young woman forced the smaller girls to give her money that she spent on chips. Now, here is an alternative statement about the same incident:

> The young woman approached the chip shop at a run. She spoke to two young girls waving her hands about. The taller of the two girls gave her some money. She went into the chip shop and came out with chips. She sat on the wall and ate the chips.

This is a more objective observation. The actual background to the incident was that:

> The mother of all three children had sent the youngest two with money for chips for all three. The oldest girl had stayed to help her mother get her grandmother into the car. She ran after her sisters and on the way she saw a friend who had moved out of the area and who had returned for a visit. She waved her arms about because she was excited about seeing her friend. The middle sister gave the elder one money for the chips which she bought and ate sitting on the wall. The others had just eaten so they did not want more chips.

Sometimes observations, even when non-judgemental, leave the observer wondering what was happening. The only way to discover this is to ask those involved. Never make assumptions. Observe young people non-judgementally, see what relationships they make, who they interact with and the skills that they show. Observe how they behave in groups. You should find that the three frameworks are helpful in identifying possible needs from your observation.

Practice your observation skills: they are fundamental to good youth work.

2. Listening to their story

Mark Smith's work is helpful here. Not many people listen to young people just because they feel their story is interesting. Most people listen to them to make decisions about their lives. Be fascinated by what the young people tell us. You are not there to pry or be told things they would rather you did not know, you are there to provide the opportunity of having someone listen to them and value them. Never push people further than they want to go.

If young people have difficulty telling you about their lives, try using some techniques such as the *River of Life*. In this method, young people are invited to draw their life as if it were a spring that develops into a stream then a river and heads for the sea. Explain that sometimes rivers run through green fields in sunshine, other times it crashes onto rocks, disappears underground and becomes invisible for a while. It can become stagnant, moving very slowly through a muddy bog. When the young person has done the drawing ask them to tell you what they want to. You may prompt with questions like 'what is happening here' but do not push to reveal things they do not wish to tell you.

Another method that works well is using an interview sheet and asking young people:

- their names
- where they live
- who are their friends
- whether they work
- what activities they enjoy
- what they would like to achieve in their lives
- what they like to be known as
- who is in their family
- whether they are in education and how they feel about it
- what are their hopes and fears

Youth workers sometimes feel that this is intrusive. Our experience is of queues of young people 'waiting to be done.' They want someone to listen to them.

One way of recording observations is to write a record divided into fact, assumption and opinion.

There are many activities you can buy, that help people learn and talk about themselves, their feelings and attitudes: for example, 'It's a Man's World,' the 'Grapevine', games and quizzes in magazines or interaction games. Try them and evaluate the results. This way you will build up a repertoire of skills in the area.

3. Doing things with them

Have fun, try new activities, talk about things that interest you, enjoy each other's company. This will give you insights into young people's interests, their view of the world, experiences and values.

4. Learning about their area

Investigate where the young people live: their school or place of work, the places they go and the things they do.

When you work with these four strands just described, only you can decide how much of the process you will share with the young person and how much they will be party to the analysis. As a rule, young people should be involved as far as possible. However the fact that the young people are not yet capable of following all the processes of need identification should not stop you planning to meet their needs.

Combining these four sources of information should give you a picture of the young person and all the areas of their need that have been discussed. You are now in a position to begin to meet these needs.

Chapter Eight

Planning a Programme

Introduction

This chapter summarises:
- The rationale and origins of programming.
- The definitions of the component parts of the programming.
- The model Youth Work Curriculum.
- Designing your own programme.

Rationale Behind the Programme

The starting point is that youth workers and youth work needs to be **proactive.** Youth workers have always taken the position that 'it is better to know more, to be able to do more and to be clearer about what you think and believe, than to remain static'. It follows that if young people are to grow and not remain static, each youth organisation needs to have a systematic planned programme, to help young people develop towards becoming **autonomous adults**, and to provide **learning experiences** to enable them to work towards agreed **objectives**.

Where Does This Programme Come From?

Its **origins** lie in six **areas**:
1. The purpose of the organisation.
2. The young people's wants and needs.
3. The skills, interests and qualifications of the workers.
4. What adults believe that young people should experience or know, be predisposed towards and able to do.
5. Local, and national, events and occasions, in which the specific youth organisation can take part.
6. The provision of equality of opportunity, and a safe learning climate.

Constructing a **programme** is the art of the possible. It is dependent on the number of staff, how and where the youth work is delivered, and, not least, resources. As with all youth work, balance is the key to success. If the programme focuses on:
- Meeting young people's **needs**, then it is an advice, counselling and information centre.

- Meeting young people's **wants**, then it is a leisure facility.
- Offering a programme based on the worker's **interests**, then it is allowing the workers to be self-indulgent.
- Things that older adults, or society in general, feel that **young people should know**, and be predisposed towards, then it will produce an environment similar to school.
- What is **available**, then there will be little coherence or direction in the work.

If the areas are blended skilfully, then the resulting programme will engage a wide range of young people and offer ways of meeting their needs. This will be equally true for all locations of youth work delivery, whether:

- voluntary youth organisations
- local authority operations
- outreach and detached work
- activity-based work

What is true for all youth work organisations, is that the development of the **origins** or themes, should be at the heart of the youth work programme. The planning of a balanced systematic programme is essential in order to offer effective learning opportunities. However, this should not be all: the experiences of spontaneity, creativity and fun are equally important areas of the programme.

Some Definitions
Autonomous adults

Autonomy is the state that an individual reaches when they have developed an ethical framework and can act on it to take control of, and be responsible for themselves and their actions. It also means that they can influence the world in which they live. Being autonomous does not mean that a person holds any particular set of beliefs. It is their ethical code and value base that determines how they act. It is possible to be an autonomous anarchist, or drug dealer, or gardener or priest.

Figure 6 shows a diagram of factors which contribute to the development in people of autonomy, in a way that is within youth service ethics. The promotion of these themes should be at the heart of the youth work programme.

Objectives

To understand how this works, think of:

- The Scouts or Guides.
- A local authority youth club in an urban area.
- A voluntary information and counselling service.

Each organisation seems very different, and each has different aims or **objectives**, yet all youth work organisations have common under-pinning factors, i.e. to promote the development of young people into autonomous individuals, which collectively define youth work.

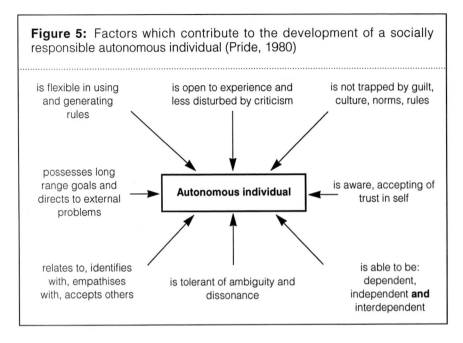

Figure 5: Factors which contribute to the development of a socially responsible autonomous individual (Pride, 1980)

Curriculum

A **curriculum** describes the whole process by which learning is offered, accepted and internalised. It also includes factors that help, or block, the process. An orgainsation's curriculum deals with such matters as:

- Getting access to the organisation.
- How needs are assessed.
- The contents of the learning.
- How the work is evaluated.
- The purpose of the organisation.
- The style in which learning is offered.
- How the learning is answered.

Syllabus

The **syllabus** refers to the subject areas that are, or can, be covered in the curriculum content. What syllabus an organisation offers will depend on the organisation's:

- Purpose.
- Resources, both human and physical.
- The young peoples' needs and wants.

Each youth work organisation has its own curriculum and syllabus that is determined by its purpose, but with a common objective, to offer learning experiences to promote autonomous individuality in young people.

The Youth Work Curriculum

This is very important. The term **youth work curriculum** has been sometimes brought into disrepute, though because of poor practice, not because the concept is faulty or irrelevant, the word curriculum conjures up memories of:

> ...school...boring lessons...learning irrelevant things.
> ...being treated like children when we knew we weren't...

and the promulgated Youth Work Curriculum has become in some places:

> Lists of things that we have to put into descriptions of our work and show that we are doing the right things.
> A document that sets out the things we should be doing, like women's issues, anti-oppressive practice, participation, empowerment, is that what you mean?

Over the years much has been written about the curriculum and the term has been defined and redefined. The trend has been to widen its meaning. The Further Education Unit's (FEU's) working definition is:

> Those processes which enhance or, if they go wrong, inhibit a person's learning...
> ...an organic process by which learning is offered, accepted and internalised.

This definition contains the key elements of the concept of curriculum:
- Curriculum is an organic process. It is not a list of subject areas, a syllabus or a Statement of Aims or Objectives.
- The process is the offering and the acceptance of learning. This does not imply that the learner is a passive receiver of learning; the process by which the learning is offered may be participative, active and through experience. However, it does imply that the learning must be offered in a way acceptable to the learner. If it is not, it will be rejected.

Learning can be made either acceptable or unacceptable by:
1. The **climate** in which it is offered. Does it feel safe or unsafe?
2. The **way** it is offered: the style, the words used, and the ethos.
3. **What** is offered: whether the learning seems relevant to the learner and whether it engages their interest.
4. The **sequence** in which it is offered: learning is made easier if it builds onto existing knowledge and skills and explores currently-held attitudes and beliefs before moving on.

The process of learning can be enhanced or inhibited by a huge range of factors that include:
- Gaining access to a place where learning is offered.
- The skill of the person facilitating the learning, which will in turn be dependent on their working situation, training, support and supervision.
- The resources available to assist the process.

Making contact

At the **central point** of the curriculum is the relationship between worker and young person which offers the young person:
- Experience of a caring, adult relationship between equals.

- A sounding board.
- An opportunity to experience, and practice, the skills of disagreeing, compromise, and laughing together.
- Stability.
- A person who is there for them.

The core of the curriculum

This is composed of:

- self awareness
- relationship building
- decision-making skills
- creating a positive self-image
- inter-personal skills
- creativity

Delivery of the curriculum

The curriculum has six **areas of its delivery**, which are wrapped together, around the core, as strands of a rope:

1. One-to-one working, befriending, giving advice, information and counselling.
2. Group work and team work: learning the skills of working together and how groups work.
3. Challenging prejudice.
4. Activities: trying new and stimulating things; experiencing personal challenges.
5. Young people's issues e.g. homelessness, substance abuse, health issues.
6. Personal, social and political education.

The whole of the Youth Work Curriculum is delivered within a framework of equal opportunities, anti-oppressive practice and the values of youth work.

The path of learning

As their relationship develops, the worker leads the young person along their individual learning pathway, by means of a series of **micro-learning circles**, see Figure 8.

Case Study: Gill

A youth worker, Wendy, sees Gill walking slowly by herself. Gill is usually with Andy. Wendy knows Gill well.

Micro Learning Circle 1

Worker's need:	To find out if Gill is all right
Intervention:	*Wendy:* 'Hi Gill. Everything OK?'
Action:	*Gill:* 'Yeah...sort of...' Gill screws up her nose and doesn't smile
Feedback:	*Wendy:* 'Want to talk about it? You seem a bit down'.
Feedback:	*Gill:* with tight smile, 'Yeah...'
Learning?	*Gill:* thinks, 'Wendy cares about me, she is offering me time'.

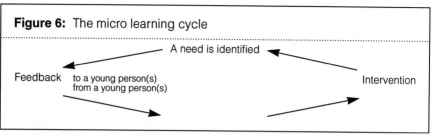

Figure 6: The micro learning cycle

Micro Learning Circle 2

Worker's Need:	To find a time and a place to talk
Intervention:	*Wendy:* 'Would you like a coffee?'
Action:	*Gill:* looks at her watch and shakes her head. 'No I've got to pick up my little sister and mind her.'
	Wendy: 'When, then?'
	Gill: 'Tonight at 8.30, at the Coffee Bar.'
Learning:	*Gill:* thinks, 'Wendy is not going to give up on me. She's flexible, she's worth talking to, but I don't trust her completely.'
Feedback:	*Wendy:* 'I'm glad I bumped into you. See you there.'
	Gill: smiles, and says, 'See you.'

The interaction is concluded. There have been two learning cycles completed in under a minute.

The Youth Work Syllabus

This is a list of subject areas that can be drawn into the Youth Work Curriculum. As already discussed, different organisations have different approaches which are determined by:

1. the organisation's terms of reference
2. the young people's needs at that time
3. what is possible and practical to offer

These will form the strands of the curriculum of the organisation and may include:

- countering prejudice
- confidence building and assertiveness
- relationship-making and building skills
- health and drugs education
- outdoor education
- developing world issues
- communication and decision making
- citizenship
- job seeking and holding
- knowing yourself
- personal effectiveness
- sex and gender education
- physical development, sport, dance
- green issues
- political education and participation
- team work, teamworking and leadership
- creative skill development
- counselling, befriending advice and information giving

- parenting skills
- first aid

- skills for life and independent living
- spirituality

Designing Your Own Programme

The role of the youth worker is to weave a programme together which will allow individuals in their target group to:

- Move towards responsibility and autonomy.
- Meet their needs, by moving groups and individuals through a personal learning pathway within the Youth Work Curriculum.
- creative skill development.

The programme should be designed to meet the needs of specific individuals and groups, by being challenging, responsive and flexible. It is artificial to separate access, delivery and content, as the curriculum as a whole is an organic process, within which are a number of elements that are bonded together and may occur simultaneously:

- Contact between the youth worker and young person.
- Development of their relationship to a point where they share feelings of trust, honesty, openness and equality as people.
- The establishment of an ethos (expectations, values and normative controls), which allows people to:
  - value learning and giving
  - support others in the process
  - try new things
  - take risks
  - 'fail', learn from the experience and try again
  - share feelings
  - work together
- Negotiations with young people to establish their learning pathway.

A check list for your programme

Finally, review your programme. Does it:

- Meet the objectives of your organisation?
- Ensure that the practice is anti-oppressive and based in equality of opportunity?
- Balance all the origins of the programme?
- Contain challenge, stimulation and the opportunity to make friends?
- Allow space for creativity, spontaneity and fun?
- Allow for a safe learning climate to develop?
- Fit into the resources that you have?
- Meet the learning needs of the young people?
- Move young people towards responsible autonomy?

Chapter Nine

Forward Planning

It is easy for a unit to drift on from week to week, just:

- following the pattern
- reacting to events
- dealing with problems
- undertaking the occasional piece of planned work

The result is usually that the workers and young people become bored, because most of the work is reactive or patterned. The purpose of planning is to move from being **re-active** to being **pro-active** and to gain some control over your work. This is an **anti-kipper strategy**.

Planning: An Anti-kipper Strategy

All this planning may seem:

> *Boring, unnecessary and part of a plot to stop us working with young people.*
> (Youth worker, Mid Glamorgan)

No, it is not, and here is why! Planning helps you to take control of your professional life. When your plans are based on good research, no one can argue against them, unless they have better research. Who knows your patch better than you? You are the expert here.

When your plans are submitted to and approved by your employers, it is hard for them to make changes to your work for their purposes. Planning puts you in a strong position. If, or when, something goes wrong, you will have evidence of your planning for the activities. This is partly why it is so important to keep copies of the risk assessments, Quality Assurance procedures, etc. Things go wrong that are not your fault, but lack of planning **is** your responsibility. Good planning protects you.

Lastly, the major reason to plan is because it results in youth work that is:

- relevant to young people's needs
- achievable and deliverable
- safe
- of high quality

Planning leads to a better deal for young people.

Starting the Forward Planning Process:

High quality research underpins all planning. The questions to ask before you start the planning processes are:

- What do I need to know?
- How can I find out this information?
- How can I ensure that the information I get is accurate?

1. *Information and data which you should have to hand*

In fact it may have never been recorded, or put somewhere safe, and seldom seen the light of day (the authors plead guilty to this). It is helpful if each unit carries up-to-date information on:

- An analysis of the social situation of the young people who are involved with the unit.
- A broad indication of the needs of the young people.
- A clear idea of the levels of resources that are available to the unit. For example:
  - Staffing: a list of workers that shows whether they are paid or voluntary, the number of contracted sessions and their individual qualifications and experience.
  - The level of clerical support.
  - Access to buildings.
  - Transport: its funding and the vehicles themselves.
  - Training opportunities, details and the available monies.
- The employing organisation's policies, procedures and practices. These should include information around:
  - health and safety
  - child protection
  - equal opportunities
  - staff development policies
  - the service's policy and standing orders (financial regulations, etc.)
  - information on government policy and practices and how it may affect the lives of young people. (e.g. how young people, who are not in work, access money and training)
  - a diary of dates that may affect the work

The diary of dates may include holidays and holiday periods, Youth Work Week, religious festivities, opportunities for young people to take part in local events, and information about community events. The diary may list when the fair is coming, race days, galas and events specifically for young people. It should also include youth work commitments, including area team meetings, unit team meetings, steering groups or management committee meetings, conferences and the dates when reports need to be completed.

If all this information is readily available, organising is far easier, and it is less likely that mistakes will be made that cause problems.

Community profiles, youth needs surveys and mapping

The process of keeping informed on the social situation of young people is continuous. Each project has to gather this information and ensure it is kept up-to-date. A **community profile** or **youth needs survey** is a systematic study of the area. One way to approach this is through questionnaires and focus groups though this does tend to produce a rather clinical description of a community to which its members might not relate. Further, it may not be an accurate reflection of their lives.

An alternative method is to immerse yourself in the community for a week, undertaking the approach shown in Figure 7.

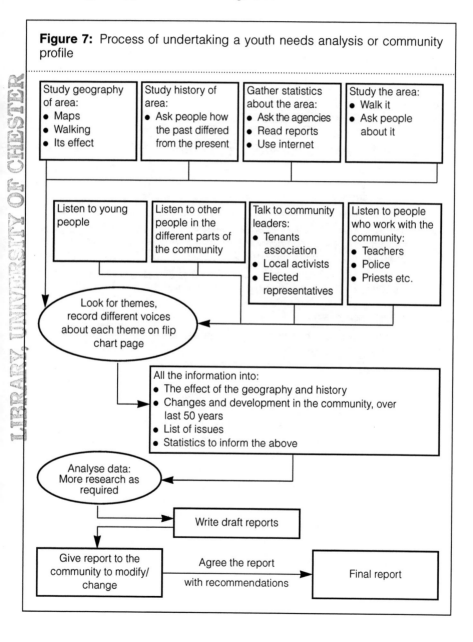

Figure 7: Process of undertaking a youth needs analysis or community profile

The advantage of this methodology, or way of working, is that it empowers the community, and builds up links between the youth workers, the community and the professionals who work with them. It begins the networking process.

Planning Tools

There are four types of planning tools that you may need:

1. A forward planning calendar and diary.
2. An Annual Plan.
3. An Action Plan.
4. A Development Plan.

1. Forward planning calendar and diary

This means a wall calendar showing when things are happening, and a desk diary that people can write in day-to-day details that other team members may need to know. Otherwise, hours and hours may be wasted:

- Looking for the letter with dates in it, that I meant to put in my diary.
- Sorting out double bookings because I had not put team meetings on the planner.
- Phoning all day trying to find out if the meeting was on Tuesday the 8th or Wednesday the 9th: she'd written Tuesday the 9th, you see.

Systematic use of a diary and wall planner can save stress and wasted time. This may seem obvious but it is surprising how often that it is forgotten.

2. The Annual Plan

The annual plan sets out the work of an organisation for the coming year. The usual framework for an Annual Plan is:

- A very short account of the area that the unit serves, and the situation of the young people.
- Bullet points of the last year's achievements.
- The themes of next year's work with the reason for these. This section ends in a statement of the community's main aim for the year.
- Each aim is taken in turn, and set out with the objectives that will enable the unit to move towards meeting the aim.
- Each objective is set out with the tasks that will be undertaken to meet the objectives. The tasks should be written so that the necessary resources are indicated, and how the quality of the work will be checked.

Note another obvious but frequently overlooked point: the total of the resources that you plan to use should not exceed the resources that you have!

Case Study: Part of an annual plan of a mobile project which travels round four large villages.

Aim: to make young people aware of how to keep themselves healthy. (This work arises from the Youth Planning group's residential weekend).

Objectives from the planning group:
- To introduce young people to the idea of healthy living in a fun way. This would take the form of a programme to run from August to the end of December.
- Run a series of events that could be repeated in each of the four major villages.
- Bring in workers from the services located in town so that the young people could meet them and get to know them.
- Link in with the Area Health Authority's 'Fit for life' programme and bid for funding for them.
- Involve young people in all stages of the work, planning, delivery and evaluation.

Method: Over the four months the following areas will be explored:
1. The importance of exercise (August).
2. Sexual Health (September/October).
3. Healthy Eating (November).
4. Substance use and abuse (November/December)

August
A week of physical activities to be run in each of the four villages, with the help of young volunteers who will be trained. The week will probably include:
- trip to swimming pool in town
- orienteering
- rounders event
- summer disco and dance event
- visits from community health action team
- first aid—ABC course

A planning group from the young people's planning group will plan the details for each village.

Costs		£
Part-time worker's sessions		
Planning with young people's group	10 sessions	
Training young volunteers (July)	10 sessions	
Planning and poster publicity with group	8 sessions	
Planning and organisation of the week	6 sessions	
Delivery of the week x 4	40 sessions	
Evaluation day for volunteers with yp	6 sessions	
Presentation events to Parish Councils	8 sessions	
	88 sessions	=1160
Materials and equipment 4 x £10		40
Hire of minibuses etc.		500
Lunch for community health		40
Fees to first aid provider (to be met centrally)		0
Certificates and presentation evening 4 x £50		200
		1940

Points for Quality Assurance
- Participants comments on daily evaluation sheets.
- Numbers participating.
- Return visits.
- Quiz to be held before the disco on 'Fit for Life' community action, will indicate what young people now know about exercise and fitness.
- Comments of community health and how they and their messages were received.
- Number of accidents.
- Volunteers' comments at the evaluation day.

3. The Action Plan

This is the detail of how each major objective, and a set of tasks from the Development Plan, are to be put into action. It sets out who does what, and where and when they do it. It also shows to whom they report, where they get help and support from, and how progress will be reviewed. The manager's job is to make sure that all the action plans work sympathetically with each other. A member of staff cannot be in two places at once! No individual should be asked to take on a heavy load week after week. Resources need checking, repairing and replacing, and this all takes time. The overall planning must take this into account.

One way to achieve this, is to produce a picture of the activity of the unit over a given time to show how the various action plans weave together. See diagram in Figure 8.

The diagram shows a plan to ensure that a project, which in this case is a youth club:
- Offers a varied programme to young people.
- Ensures that activities are spread out in a way that does not overload workers or resources.
- Ensures that each worker has an opportunity to develop their interests and allows the centre to have 'highlights' that everyone can build up to and share.

Catching Activities: these draw young people into the centre. This might include outreach work, 'come and try it' events, open discos or advertising programmes.

Holding Activities: are things which young people enjoy and can do with minimal worker involvement: coffee bar, snooker, pool, music room or outdoor sports area, but which workers can use as tools for their work.

Runners: are activities that take place occasionally but regularly: youth forums, football team, adventure weekends.

Short Projects: are designed to involve young people in a new, stimulating and challenging project. They give individuals or groups of workers the opportunity to undertake pieces of work:

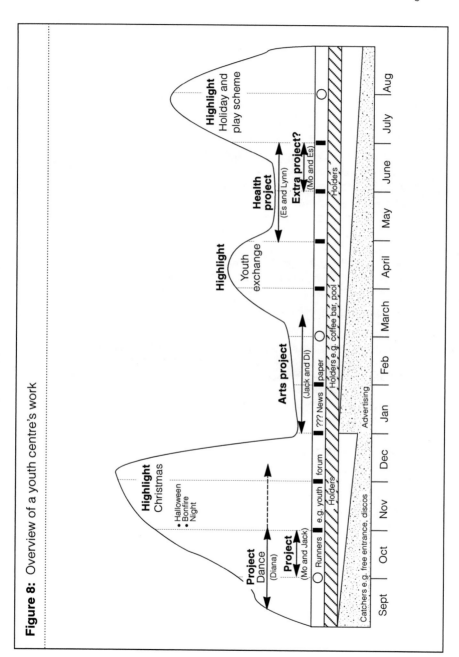

Figure 8: Overview of a youth centre's work

- With a beginning, middle and end.
- That reflect their interests and concerns.
- That are focused on specific groups and their needs.
- That develop both themselves and the young people.

Highlights: these are major events in the year that involve everyone. They are multi-stranded, for example Christmas can involve:
- Performances given in hospitals or care homes.
- Fundraising for an organisation that works with homeless people.
- A Christmas event for the elderly.
- Christmas shopping for people with reduced mobility.
- Making cards and presents.
- Decorating the meeting space.
- A religious event.
- A party or disco.

Highlights give the year structure. They often become part of a ritual and they draw people together, as everyone is involved in a common theme.

4. The Development Plan

This is a plan that sets out the long view for the development of a unit or organisation. It usually begins with a vision of where the project will be in three or five years time, and the steps the organisation intends to take towards that vision. It contains the background to, and present state of, the organisation or unit. Evidence that supports the reason for the direction that the organisation or unit has decided to take, might include.
- the vision
- the aim
- details of the developmental stages including intended actions for each stage
- the financial plan
- legal considerations
- staff training implications
- processes for the managing of, consulting about and quality control of the process
- targets for level of use of the changed and developed services
- indicators for the initial steps of the development plan
- a review process

Chapter Ten

Monitoring, Evaluation, Assessment and Recording Work

The purpose of this chapter is to explore the areas of monitoring, evaluation, assessment and recording, in order to equip you to critically review your work and to produce evidence of your activities when this is required. It should also be helpful in managing your boundaries, making cases for resources and informing your manager of the details of what you are doing. They will be able to use the information in turn to explain the value of the service and argue for further resources.

Some Definitions:

Monitoring is the process of gathering information and evidence about an educational process.

Recording is making a permanent record. Records can be written, photographed, tape recorded or captured on video. The record may be made by youth workers or young people, by individuals or groups.

Assessment is a method of reviewing performance against pre-set criteria.

Evaluation is the process of reviewing movement towards achieving the objectives. It considers a wide range of factors: anything that effected the movement. Monitoring and indicators helps in this process.

There are two **types** of evaluation:

1. **Formative evaluation** takes place during a piece of work and answers the questions:
   - 'Where are we?'
   - 'How did we get here?'
   - 'What did we learn on the way?'
   - 'What do we do now to move towards our objectives?'
2. **Summative evaluation** takes place at the end of a piece of work and answers the questions:
   - 'Did we reach our objectives?'
   - 'Why was this?'
   - 'What happened that helped or blocked this?'
   - 'What have we learned?'
   - 'What recommendation do we want to make to others who tread this path?'

It might appear that there is a third type of evaluation, though more accurately it is an assessment:

3. **Competencies** is a description of skills that can be demonstrated and assessed against a given set of criteria that have been previously agreed and explained,

but there are difficulties with assessment of competency, which will be dealt with later.

About Evaluation

Evaluation: Don't know. We do it but I'm never very sure what good it does. I mean, the young people say all sorts of things like:
 – Kev's socks smelled.
 – Lets do it again soon.
Then we write something down and put it in a file and it never sees the light of day again...

Beware of evaluation becoming just a description of an unplanned session with young people, where the sole purpose was 'To see how it went'. For evaluation to be effective it must be built into the planning process.

Evaluation should take place by comparing achievements with the planned objectives. If you don't know what you are trying to do, it is impossible to work out if you did it or not! The nature of the objectives will determine the methods of monitoring and recording, which should be decided before a piece of work starts. These processes can then begin at the start of the work, thus avoiding people trying to remember what happened, and disagreeing about it.

Young people's involvement in the evaluation process requires their active and informed participation. Young people may need to learn appropriate skills such as identifying their own achievement and learning, and that of others. These skills may need to be taught as part of their learning programme. Monitoring, evaluation and recording can and should be part of the learning process.

There are two **styles** of evaluation, qualitative and quantitative.

Qualitative evaluation

This refers to evaluation of the quality of the learning and how those involved experienced it. It is subjective, for example:
 • How people felt about what happened?
 • Which were the best or worst or most significant experiences?

These questions may appear to be measurable in that people can mark themselves off on a scale, e.g.:

Not Confident 0 —— 1 —— 2 —— 3 —— 4 —— 5 Confident

Put X where you feel you were at the beginning of the year.
Put O where you feel you are now

But really they are subjective because they involve self-assessment. Nevertheless, qualitative evaluation is useful as it explores people's perceptions of events and of their development. Further, if several people from different backgrounds share a common perception then it is more likely to be true than one person's view.

For example, put an X where you think Chris was three months ago, and put an O where you think he is now:

Less thoughtful	0——1——2——3——4——5	more thoughtful
Less excitable	0——1——2——3——4——5	more excitable
Less good at listening	0——1——2——3——4——5	better at listening

If six people all think that Chris moved significantly from being less good at listening to being better at listening then this is likely to be true. The more different their individual situations the greater the strength of evidence.

The common area of perception can be seen against very different life experiences. Note b and c are long standing best friends and they have much in common.

The subjective evidence can be confirmed by evidence from recordings: photographs, anecdotes and written material.

> Two months ago Chris never remembered what people said, but on Thursday in the message taking game Chris remembered all that stuff George said to him.

> When Karrina was upset it was Chris who got her some tea and talked with her. A few months ago we all said that Chris never seemed to care how we felt: thats a big difference isn't it.

Quantitative evaluation

This refers to the evaluation of that element of the learning that can be measured. It is objective and might include such things such as:

- The attendance of individuals.
- The length of time over which individuals attended.
- The age and gender of the participants.

Such measurements can be extended to competencies.

About competencies

As we saw above, these are descriptions of knowledge, understanding and skills which people can demonstrate e.g.:

- Name three types of feedback.
- Describe the effect on the recipient, of each of these types of feedback.
- Demonstrate the giving of two types of feedback.

Assessing by competencies sounds like the ideal monitoring tool as it gives measurable outcomes. There is nothing subjective about meeting these competencies: either you can do it, or you can't. Would it were as simple as this. There are major difficulties in using competencies as the sole method of assessment, mainly because the precise writing of competencies is difficult. If they are too prescriptive, there are administrative difficulties; if they are too loose, then they are worthless. One example is assessing the ability to phone a local railway station and inquire the time of a train to another major town to arrive by 6 p.m.

The assessment sounds clear enough but does it mean that the person has to:

1. Do it:
- – at the first time of asking OR
- – with encouragement and support OR
- – in not more than three attempts OR
- – when not under pressure OR
- – when under pressure?

2. Remember the information, and if so, for how long?

3. Be able to write down the information?

and are these last two points exploring different competencies?

Evaluation by competencies considers skills one at a time, but things that you can do in a calm situation became far harder in a complex one.

A major skill of youth workers, as has been discussed, is that the individuals use themselves as a tool for delivering youth work. This requires a process of continual monitoring. What is happening to the young people with whom you are working? You must assess how they are reacting, and modify your style and way of working to allow for this. Writing competencies for such an assessment is hard and it is even harder to assess. It is particularly difficult to write or assess competencies in areas of creativity. The process of writing competencies is essentially an analytical skill, which is the very opposite of creativity. This raises a dilemma, is it possible to analyse creativity?

Competencies can produce in learners a state of mind that says 'Crossed that off: done it'. When this is the case, the skill that has been demonstrated may not become integrated into the person's practice.

Competency-based assessment can feel barren, devoid of excitement, enthusiasm and excellence. It has been referred to as 'paralysis by analysis'.

Competencies are undoubtedly useful. They can offer a systematic and fair approach to assessment, clarity concerning the skills that people are expected to demonstrate in their work, and a way of evaluating the offering of learning:

- Did the learning offer, and provide, reasonable opportunities for learners to develop the skills to demonstrate the competencies?
- Was the method of assessment one that ensures that people have practical skills, as well as the skills to describe or write about a subject?

It shows that you can do it.

Recording: The Easy Way

Writing about your work can be quite daunting. This is especially so if you have done little writing since you left school and are unused to recording systematically. It is important however, that all work and good practice are recorded.

How to move forward? If writing and recording are regarded as a skill then they can be set in the context of other specialist youth work skills. Not everyone is expected to be an outdoor education worker or to have skills in arts, craft and drama. Most teams have at least one person who is good at putting ideas together in a systematic way on paper. There is also usually someone who enjoys word processing and can set out the words in an attractive and accessible manner. If the youth worker has a framework, or set of questions, to help them to describe and reflect on their work, then recording becomes a team activity.

1. The worker asks the questions.
2. The team records the answers into a dictation machine.
3. The word processor types them.
4. The writer puts the words into shape.
5. Each speaker checks out the result to see that their words haven't become distorted in the process.

It is to be hoped that, once people are involved in the recording process they will become more confident and competent at it. Producing recordings should be part of people's paid work rather than done in their own time.

The person producing the plan, report or evaluation should be the one who organises the agreeing of the framework. If it is an evaluation, then the questions will be agreed in the planning process, because it is a good idea for each unit to have a record of good practice. In this case, every worker should record two pieces of good work a year using the framework set out below:

- What led you to do the piece of work?
- What was the purpose?
- Give a thumbnail sketch of the young people involved, bearing in mind confidentiality.
- What needs were you seeking to meet?
- How did you identify these needs?
- What did you plan to do?
- What happened?
- What were the learning outcomes for all those involved?
- Include photographs, or other recordings, that offer readers a flavour of the experience.

Chapter Eleven

Introduction to Boundary, Time and Stress Management

Shula, a youth worker who runs a youth club on a school campus and works with young people at risk of being excluded said:

> I've got a funny relationship with the school. See that group over there? Well, I do the Duke of Edinburgh's Award at lunch time and when they got their Silver, it came out in the press as a school achievement. When the same group messed about on motorcycles in the car park after school and the neighbours complained, they were youth club members waiting to come in to the club in two hours time!
>
> Then last month, the PE teachers started to send all the year 7s who hadn't kit for games over to the youth club! I said I couldn't be responsible for them and they couldn't use the youth club stuff (you know, the pool table, coffee bar, music system and all that) without some sort of supervision. The deputy head got all stroppy. I explained that they are all under 13 and that they couldn't even come into the club at night until they are in year 9. If things get broken the members would go mad and I'd have to sort it all out. He said, 'What's the point of having a club and a youth worker if we can't use them when we need them?' I thought of trying to explain to him what my job is but it all seemed pointless. The next week, they said we couldn't use the sports hall. We used to have it one night a week, but now it's let to an adult football team.
>
> …It's constant aggravation…it takes so long to sort it all out. When I'm doing that I'm not doing the really important things, like working with the young people who are on the point of being excluded.
>
> It winds me up…but some of the teachers are really fantastic. I often blow off steam to Mrs Grant: she's told me to see my boss about it and to try to get him to sort it out with the head. She does what she can to keep it all calm, but it gets me down and the amount of time it takes makes me angry.
>
> I'm working fourteen sessions a week, what with the club; the young people in trouble at school; the lunch time club and a bit of personal, social and health education (PSHE). All my manager can say is 'Well, work less in the school holiday. Take time off in lieu (TOIL) then.' That's no good. We should be available to the kids in the holidays. When do I take my leave? I'm absolutely knackered and half term isn't for another week.

This worker's story is a familiar one. Too many youth workers, both full and part-time are:

- Regularly working well over their contracted hours, often because they feel a sense of duty to the young people. After all they came into youth work to 'grow' young people.

- Trying to manage relationships with a range of organisations (inter-agency working), without clear boundaries being established, before the work started. The result is they have to resolve things as they go along.
- Coping with young people whose behaviour is challenging without the necessary back up, resources or support.

Consequently they are stressed and exhausted. Stressed workers are not effective.

To be effective, workers must manage three areas:

- boundary
- stress
- time

They must also manage assertively.

It sounds so easy, but is very difficult to do in practice.

> *Of course I can see what other people should do: if they ask I can help them. I just can't seem to do it for myself: it feels as if my work is constantly in chaos.*
> (Level 3 JNC full-time youth worker, based in a school)

The dilemma of youth workers is that we came into the job to help support and grow young people and their communities. If people need us, we can't say no. The result is that we become exhausted and stressed, and start to be ineffective. When we are in the eye of the storm we are so busy coping that we lose sight of the bigger picture. It then becomes easier not to think but just to plod on. The result is that we become more exhausted. These factors add together to trap us, and keep us trapped.

The rest of this section aims to help you to escape. It will describe each of the areas and how to manage them, so that you remain in control of your work and relatively 'unkippered.'

Chapter Twelve

Boundary Management

Why is it Necessary to Manage the Boundaries?

It is essential to control your work in order to manage your time and reduce the level of stress. The theory of **boundary management** provides a framework by which you can explore your work and the forces acting on you.

This understanding puts you in a position to make decisions about your work; thus you are in greater control. Good boundary management can:

- help you work more effectively
- reduce the stress
- help you to develop networks
- provide professional and personal support
- offer a way of raising the status of young people

Boundary management: the theory

No-one's job is limitless, we all have boundaries that define:

- what work we do
- where and when we work
- who we work with
- how we deliver that work

Youth and community work may appear to be more difficult than other jobs to 'tie down,' but it is essential for your effectiveness and well being that you do so.

Defining your Boundaries

Think of these limits to your work as a set of concentric circles as in Figure 9.

In order to manage your boundaries you have to know where they are. To discover this you need to:

- Read your job description carefully and consider what each statement means for the work that you do.
- If necessary, clarify your job description with your line manager.
- Discuss and agree with your line manager the ways that you will deliver work required by your job description for a period, say the next four to six months. This should be a normal part of management supervision.
- Understand the documents that act as boundaries to your work. These will include:
  - The policy of the organisation for which you work including:
  - Any specific policy documents or statements of purpose relating to youth work.
  - Policies on equal opportunities or anti-oppressive practice.

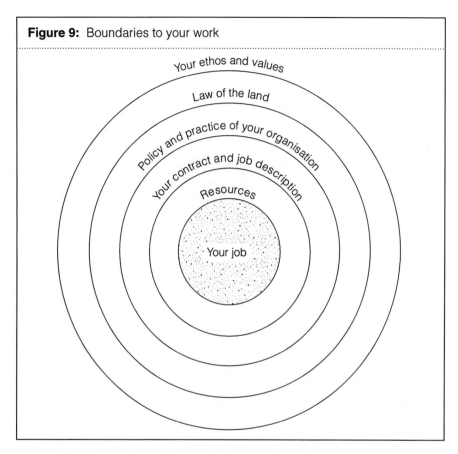

Figure 9: Boundaries to your work

Your ethos and values

Law of the land

Policy and practice of your organisation

Your contract and job description

Resources

Your job

– Child protection policy, regulations and practices.
– Health and safety policies, regulations and practices.
– Financial regulations, procedures and practices.

These documents should be explained to you as part of the induction to your job. If no one has discussed them with you, or you do not understand how any part of them affects your work, then ask your line manager. You need to know, because if something goes wrong then these documents could well be the basis of any investigation. If you cannot get the help you need then take advice from your union. If you are not a union member, consider joining!

Some notes to help you to evaluate your job description

Both paid and voluntary workers should have a job description. It is the document that describes the work that you are contracted to undertake. It should set out:

- Your job title.
- Your place of work.

- To whom you are accountable.   • For whose work you are responsible.
- The current key tasks of your post.• The limits to your authority.

There may be a final statement, that is a catch-all, that will read something like:

> *To undertake any duties that may be required from time to time that are consistent with the duties and status of the post and which are agreed by the postholder.*

Roughly speaking you cannot be asked to do anything which:

- Contradicts the purpose of the post.
- Requires regular work that is usually done by someone more senior or junior to your post.
- Takes more than 10–15 per cent of your time.

If the additional duties take longer than this and they are a permanent part of the work, then it can be considered a change in your job description for which your agreement is required.

Two further points:

1. It is helpful if there is an indication of priorities within the key tasks, and the percentage of time that you are expected to spend on each task.

   For example:

   At least...sessions a week will be face-to-face work (JNC 2 worker).

   As a part-time worker in charge of the project you will use one session a week for administration and planning.

   The training element of the post will not exceed 25 per cent of your time.

2. Make sure that your job description can be undertaken. Ensure that all the elements of your job description are in place and that the job is realistic and achievable. Remember: it is the legal document that defines your job. The boundary set by your job description will be far wider than the work you can actually undertake in the number of sessions or hours that you are employed. This is why you should agree with your manager the parts of the job description that you are to implement over the next four to six months.

Case Study: Job description for a newly created post

> You are taking up a newly created post. Your job description says that you will work on North End Estate and a key task is:
> *To make contact with young people 14–16 years who are at risk of exclusion from school, and to work with them to reduce this risk and to offer social and emotional education.*
>
> You calculate that there are some 180 young people who fall into this category. You then need to agree with your manager or supervisor:
>
> - How will you go about this task? Detached work on the estate? Referrals from school; social services; YOT?
> - How many young people is it reasonable to expect you to work with in any one period of time?
> - What happens if any young people contact you when they should be in school?

- Where is the work on social and emotional education to be undertaken and what resources are available to you for this?
- What prior work has been done with the schools and their staff? Do they know you exist? Are they in agreement with the work that you are going to do? Whom should you relate to within the school?
- What percentage of your overall time should be spent on this task?

If you do not get your boundaries defined before you begin the work you will run into all sorts of difficulties that could help 'kipper' you, see Figure 10.

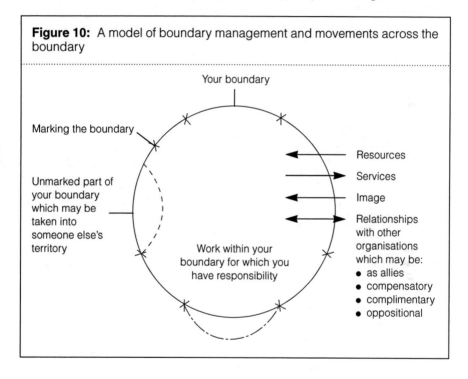

Figure 10: A model of boundary management and movements across the boundary

The Principles of Boundary Management

1. Accept responsibility for everything that happens within your boundary.
2. Mark your boundary so others know where it lies. Make sure that you are the one to manage the four movements across your boundaries to and from the 'outside world':
   - resources   - services
   - image   - relationships
3. Never let anyone add to your boundaries or remove pieces of your boundary without your agreement.

Accepting responsibility for everything that happens inside your boundary

Everything that happens in your territory is your responsibility. This is still the case even if someone you manage, paid or voluntary, does something without your knowledge or agreement. If you do not accept responsibility, it leaves the way open for others to do so. When this happens, the area in question has moved outside your boundary, inside their boundary and into their territory.

Case Study: Iftikhar

> **Iftikhar** was taking a small group into an adult education centre to use the computer suite. It was the first time they had done this. The young people were excited to be in a new place. As they crossed the foyer they began to push and shove and laugh loudly. The manager of the centre came out of his office with a look on his face that said, 'I am going to stamp my authority here.'
>
> If he had done so he would have asserted his power over **how** the young people came in, and later perhaps, over **who** came in.
>
> Iftikhar moved ahead of the group and faced the manager. He smiled and said, 'I am so sorry, we'll try that again.' He turned round, spread his arms wide and ushered the group outside. After a quick word in the car park, the group came back in quietly. The manager came out of his office and said 'Welcome to the Woodlodge Centre, enjoy yourselves.'
>
> Iftikhar's use of his skills meant that the management of and work with the young people was left within his boundary whilst the manager was left to manage the centre.

When something goes wrong within your boundary, as inevitably it will, do not ignore the matter. Deal with it and be seen to accept responsibility. This is a major skill area. The method which people seem to find works best is to:

- Turn up in person, especially if you judge the matter to be serious, or you are in sole charge, and even if this is inconvenient. It shows how seriously you take the situation. Never hide behind someone you manage. If you manage the person most closely involved in what went wrong, empower them to deal with the matter. Do not depower them by taking things out of their hands unless it is critical. Give them support and help them work out an action plan.
- Do not jump to conclusions and make judgements. Listen to what everyone has to say and then try to work out what happened, and why, before you do anything.
- Do not put down or show up anyone, including those you manage. Be supportive. No one feels good about getting something wrong.
- When you are sure that you know the full facts about the situation, do what is necessary to resolve it. This may include apologising and informing your manager.
- When emotions have died down, review the situation in a way that everyone learns from the outcomes.
- Write whatever reports are required.

Marking your boundaries regularly

An unmarked boundary rapidly becomes invisible. You might mark your boundary by such things as:

- Designing a house style for all your written material. You may need to take advice from someone who is good with computers and the relevant software, or use a professional printing company to do the work. Your organisation may have procedures that mean that you have to use their graphics designer. Check whether or not this is the case. The house style needs to be easily identifiable as yours. This should include a print style, colour scheme and logo.
- Devising a sentence or set of words that summarise the things that you do. It should be in a form that anyone can understand. Consult widely in order to get the best statement. It may be with you for a long time! Some examples of this are:

    Southfields Young Women's Project: Helping young women 13–25 to become confident, effective and to follow their star.

    Oakland Youth Centre: having fun and learning together.

    Riverside Gay Lesbian and Bi-sexual Youth Project: counselling, support, friendship and fun. Confidentiality assured.

- Extending the house style to produce:
    - business cards
    - posters
    - A5 leaflets for information for other agencies, libraries, councillors, funders etc.
    - advertising material for young people
    - lists of key achievements in the last year
- Introduce yourself to anyone, and everyone, who may be interested in your work. You may do this by writing to them and enclosing a hand out, or calling on them and inviting them to visit your place of work. People you contact may include:
    - Policy and decision makers: councillors, management committee, steering group members.
    - Community organisations: Citizens Advice Bureaux; tenants associations.
    - Agencies who work with young people: schools, social services, probation services, juvenile justice, voluntary organisations.

The effect of this is to get your boundaries known and to begin the process of relationship-building and networking. Managing movements across your boundaries, in other ways, will be looked at in more detail in Chapter 12.

Never letting anyone alter your boundaries without your agreement

In Shula's case, at the beginning of the last chapter, there were two examples of this:

1. Expecting the worker to cope with the pupils without PE kit extended the work significantly.
2. The school claiming the Duke of Edinburgh's Awards successes moved this area of work outside the worker's boundary.

Never accept your boundaries being changed, without putting up a fight. It is easy to think 'If I say anything it won't make any difference in the end and I'll just get a reputation as a trouble maker'. It is only later that you complain to others about how unfair it is. Remember! If you behave like a door mat, then you will be treated like one. It is always worth pointing out what the effects of the change of boundary will have on your resources, such as:

- you and your colleague's time
- staffing
- training and support
- supervision of staff
- the other work that you do

Put these points in writing, if discussion has no effect. It may cause a rethink, and, if anything happens in the future, you can always show that you did point out the problems before the changes occurred. It is useful to keep a record of even small changes of your boundary. A number of small changes can add up to a significant change. You may be in a position to make a case for:

- more resources
- a change in your job description
- a regrading

You owe it to the people you work with, and to yourself, to find the time to manage your boundary tightly.

Boundaries and your Personal Ethical Framework and Values

We all have personal boundaries. These are defined by our beliefs and values. As a worker it is important for you to know where you stand on a whole range of issues because at times, they will not sit comfortably with the formal boundaries of the job. You need to be clear about your personal beliefs and the risks you are prepared to take.

Personal beliefs

- Why you are a youth worker.
- How much you are prepared to let youth work affect your personal life. This includes the time that you spend with your family and the relationships that you have with them. Your work can leave you so emotionally drained that these relationships suffer.
- How you feel about such matters as:
  - Abortion.
  - Eating meat.
  - Using animals for testing purposes.
  - Pacifism, war and arms sales.
  - Your areas of prejudice (we all have them) and how you will handle them.
  - Areas in which you are personally vulnerable. We all have unresolved things that happened in our past, which can pop up again and catch us by surprise.

You need to be clear about where you stand in order to manage your boundaries effectively. Youth work is a generalism that covers a huge range of subjects. It follows that it is quite easy for any one to be asked to do something that makes them feel very uncomfortable. For example, a pacifist might find it difficult to attend a Remembrance Day Service on behalf of their organisation. Equally, a vegetarian may not wish to be involved in situations where meat is cooked.

If you can indicate to your manager the boundaries between your personal and professional life, it may be easier for your manager to avoid any problems that might arise.

The level of risks that you are prepared to take:

There may be a conflict between your personal beliefs and the way you are required to work, for example, between the laws on illegal substances, and the way you feel is most effective to work with young people who use them. There is no simple way of managing problems such as this. In making your decision, you need to be aware that no-one can give you permission to break the law of the land. Neither can you be given permission to go against the policy and regulations of your employer, or to exceed your job description. You may choose to do so but be aware that your actions can lead to disciplinary procedures, dismissal or even criminal charges. Having said this it may be impossible to work with the young people that you are targeting without putting yourself at some risk, such as when working with young people who carry, use and sell drugs.

There is no easy way out of these dilemmas. You can:

* Ignore the problem and run the risk of disciplinary action or imprisonment.
* Cease to work with these young people when they carry drugs and risk them deciding not to work with you.
* Spread the risk by discussing it with your managers. It is possible that you may be instructed to stop the work.

Institutional or organisational imbalances

Clashes between personal values and organisational values are not always as clear cut and potentially catastrophic as this. Common tensions include:

* Not being managed in the same way that you are being asked to work with young people i.e. participatively, openly and honestly, with a concern for their development.
* Your employing organisation being more concerned about returns, statistics and reports than the actual work with young people.
* New health and safety regulations acting as a block to things that you have done with young people before, and in some cases, many times before.
* The organisation not approving of things that happen as young people begin to take responsibility for organising activities, for example, when youth forums begin to campaign effectively on issues that concern it.
* Institutional racism, sexism or homophobia.

Only you can decide when these matters cease to be an irritant and become a point of principle on which you feel you have to make a stand. Only you can decide if making a stand is worth it. Your choice of action is limited to:

- Ignoring the problem and learning to live with it.
- Making a stand.
- Finding a job in an organisation whose beliefs and values fit more closely with how you feel the world should be. If this is possible, this is the only safe solution.

If you do decide to make a stand then there are some points that are worth considering before you do so:

- If it comes to it, are you prepared to leave your job?
- Can you cope with the levels of hassle and stress that may result from your stand? What impact will this have on your family?
- Where can you get support: colleagues, unions, other organisations?
- How can you make your stand on your terms rather than being pressured into action by outside forces?
- Have you always acted in line with your organisation's policies, instructions and codes of practice? If you have not, then you are very vulnerable.
- Have you solid evidence to support your case?
- Have you been through all the steps set out by your organisation to bring the matter formally to their attention? These will probably include raising the matter in supervision and using the grievance procedure.

Finally, if you do decide to go ahead, be aware there may be no quick solution: matters may drag on for months or even years. One way of dealing with this may be to set yourself clear and realistic targets about what you can achieve in a given period and to work towards these.

Case Study: Gwen's lack of a base

Gwen was a detached worker appointed to work with homeless young people. Her base was a desk in a busy youth office.

After two months in post she was sure that she needed a different base to:

- Meet individual young people.
- Work with small groups.
- Store paperwork, equipment and clothes for young people.
- Meet with workers in other agencies towards whom she sign-posted young people.

Her employers agreed that she did need a base, but said that they had no money to provide one.

After a year Gwen was sure that the lack of the base was seriously compromising her work. She wrote several reports saying this. In the absence of a response from her manager, Gwen found a room in a voluntary organisation. This worked well. When her manager discovered the arrangement, she was asked to move out as there were no monies for rent or insurance. Gwen decided to take grievance procedures against her employer on the grounds that 'they failed to manage her work effectively'.

Five years, and six inadequate bases later, she gave up the struggle and resigned. The experience adversely affected her health and family life.

Her achievement was demonstrated when the post was advertised later and an adequate base was offered...

Case Study: Ian's mobile unit that wasn't...

Ian took up a new post as a rural youth worker, working out of a mobile youth centre that was a large trailer on the back of a bus. His role was to serve the 18 villages and hamlets that had no youth work provision, and little public transport.

Ian began to develop the job well. He fitted into the different communities and after four months had several exciting projects running involving about 150 young people in all. He also set up a regular round with the bus, and was in contact with over 800 young people in the villages. The only problem was that the mobile was totally unreliable. The tractor unit kept breaking down, the lighting on the bus was intermittent, and the generator failed on a regular basis.

Ian was a keen cyclist and so resorted to cycling to the villages when the mobile broke down. Local people realised the problem and soon he had access to several pavilions on sports pitches and three village halls. As winter approached this way of working became impractical, so he approached his manager who said 'I'm sure that the problems with the mobile were just teething trouble. It'll be fine.' It was not. Ian wrote several reports, but still nothing happened. Finally Ian, on the advice of his union, started a grievance procedure against his employers on the grounds of their 'failing to manage his work resources effectively.'

At the hearing with his line manager's manager, Ian was amazed at how sympathetically he and his union representative were received. The senior manager's view was 'if we need the post, we need to make it work.'

Ian was asked to produce a report on his work indicating where and when the mobile should be used and the times when the village halls and pavilions worked better. He was offered:

- Bike mileage!
- A budget for project work.
- A mobile phone.
- Guaranteed part-time worker support.
- Essential car user status and the option of a car.
- A budget for renting accommodation.

His job title was changed to 'Rural Youth Work Co-ordinator' and he was asked to set up a Youth Committee to ensure that 'the rural voice was heard'.

After the hearing he said 'I was so scared, I thought they'd think I was just making waves. Now it's sorted I feel great. If I'd not gone through these procedures nothing would have happened. It's been worth all the stress.'

Managing your boundaries is a difficult task that needs constant attention: don't give up, record your successes and good luck!

Chapter Thirteen

Managing Movements Across
Your Boundaries

If you refer to Figure 10, the diagram of boundary management, you will see that four items move across your boundaries:

1. Resources.
2. Services.
3. Your image.
4. Relationships and alliances.

1. Resources

Most workers seek to draw more **resources** inside their boundary into their project. This can range from writing to factories for 'off cuts' for craft work, to making bids to a number of funders for many thousands of pounds. Be aware that drawing in funding can distort your boundaries because the money comes with strings attached:

- Funders may specify targets in terms of the numbers of young people that you should work with, in a given time. This can limit or distort your work.
- The monitoring and record-keeping you must do may include names, addresses, and progress of individuals. This can be very time consuming.
- It may be that the type of work that you do is specified. Political education and campaigning can be viewed unfavourably by funders.
- The values of the funder may differ from those of your organisation.
- Some projects may require several different funding regimes to be issued. They may all have differing monitoring requirements or require different types of outputs.

All these factors can alter the work that you do and this alters your boundaries. Be very sure that accepting the funding is worth it before you commit yourself and your organisation.

The development of the *Connexions Service* has implications for youth work in this respect. *Connexions* is partly about drawing excluded young people into existing mainstream society. It does this by trying to get young people into education, training and jobs. It is about young people reaching their potential through this type of conformity. Up until now, the youth service has usually taken the view that young people are very inexperienced young adults. The aim of *Connexions* is that they should be given the best available information on which to make decisions about their lives. They may make bad decisions on occasions, in which case they need help and support to find an alternative path. The bottom line is that it is their life, and it is they who live with the consequences. This is not usually the view of other organisations.

2. Services

The **services** referred to are those which you offer other agencies and which they offer you. They are not the services you provide for the users of your unit. Sometimes the services are paid for in money and sometimes in kind. Here are some examples of this:

> *There's this smashing guy who came to us on a three month secondment from the local TEC. He's a computer whiz and he's sorted out all the club's Internet problems and has worked with young people on their CVs and did job-ready skills with them. The TEC thinks its great 'cos it's free training for some of their staff.*
> (Part-time worker in charge of a rural youth project)

> *The school lets us drive their bus to get us to places. We just pay for the petrol. I do the occasional residential or camping trip with them in exchange when they can't find a female member of staff.*   (Detached team leader)

> *We have students on placement from the university. It's hard work and the universities are hopeless at the paperwork but it's worth it because of the energy and ideas the students bring. It keeps us on our toes!*   (Information centre manager)

> *We take part in research for the health authority because they pay us for it. We use the money to improve the facilities here.*   (Counselling agency)

This process of supplying and receiving services is important, because it enables things to happen that otherwise couldn't be done and helps build relationships between individuals and organisations. It is part of networking. This traditional way of working now has a far more commercial side.

Other agencies recognise that youth workers have skills such as being able to make contact and build relationships with difficult-to-reach young people. They can offer learning to young people that is relevant to their lives in a way that the young people can accept.

These agencies may want youth workers to use these skills to meet the agency's objectives. Schools involve youth workers in Personal Social and Health Education (PSHE) classes. Local authorities invite youth workers to help in inclusion projects. Youth Offending Teams, education welfare and careers services all want workers with youth work skills.

Youth workers often undertake this work as a part of their paid work. Their opinions differ on this:

> *Kids are kids. It doesn't matter where we work with them. Working in schools is just another place to work, and it's a great way to get to know them quickly. Of course it's different. We've just got something to offer that schools want. It's what we've always wanted: professional recognition.*

> *If other people come into school they are paid. There's a peripatetic music teacher and a basketball coach from a local professional club who both come in to do things. They get paid: I don't. I don't want the money for me, I want it*

for the service as formal recognition of the value I add to the school's curriculum. If the youth service was paid for my time, they could put in someone to replace some of my sessions on a permanent basis. I know the work I do is good, I can see the kids changing. They can see it: the school keeps saying how well its working, I think they are just using the youth service.

I said, 'No, I don't want to work in school. I've got a job that is already more than full-time. I came to do it and I'm going on doing it. Anyway the school has a different agenda to me, they don't really want to empower kids.

We train part-time workers well. They are good on the whole. Then other agencies take them on and pay them quite well. Good luck to them: I can't blame them for taking on full-time work. But why should we put in all that effort and time to run a training course and support them, when they (the other agencies) benefit more or less as soon as they've qualified? It's great for the worker's development but does us no good at all.

As a worker you have to make up your own mind where you stand on this issue.

3. Image

Whether you realise it or not, anyone who knows about you and your work will form an opinion of it. Their opinion is often not formed on accurate information. It can result from rumour, speculation or misrepresentation. An example of this, is the views of people about an excellent youth project on a deprived estate nearby:

Yes, there is a youth thing up there. I don't know what it's like. It can't be much good, I've never heard much about it.

All the dossers and druggies seem to know the workers...They all look the same...I don't see why we pay people to hang about with that lot.

All I know is I won't let my daughter go there. It's not well run...all that lot goes there.

The opinions of those interviewed is that the project was:
- for 'undesirables'
- ineffective
- badly run

These views were not based on fact. People had no information, so they made assumptions to fit their own individual prejudices. The workers had not managed the **image** of the project well, even though the work was good. This is not a plea for 'spin doctors' and news management! However, it is a reason to ensure that everyone can access up-to-date and accurate information about your work, so they can form an opinion based on fact. To achieve this, you need to:

- Make time to identify and see key people to tell them about your work, the difficulties and the successes.
- Produce a mobile display and circulate it round the public library, shopping centre, education office and schools.
- Produce information sheets, handouts and posters for shops, hairdressers, doctors and dentists surgeries, Citizens Advice Bureaux, anywhere that people will see them.

- Circulate your annual report widely: make sure that it does credit to the project and the young people.
- Produce a list of achievements over the last six months or year. Circulate this widely.
- Contact the press officer of your organisation to make sure that they do a press release on all 'good news' information. Make photo opportunities wherever possible.
- Always make yourself available to respond to any criticisms of or problems with issues inside your boundary.

All this links closely with marking your boundaries. It may seem like a lot of work if you already feel overstretched. You may also feel as if it is taking you away from working with young people. However, it is worthwhile because when you build a positive image it:

- Increases your credibility. This credibility will assist you in advocating for and on behalf of young people and youth work.
- Strengthens your networks.
- Makes help and support more readily available when you need it.
- Often makes funding easier to obtain and develop.

4. Relationships and Alliances

All organisations need to develop **relationships** with other organisations outside their boundaries. No organisation can stand completely alone. There are ranges of different reasons to establish links:

- To make a power base.
- To aid information flow.
- To provide workers with an external source of support.
- For the benefit of young people.
- To prevent duplication of effort and encourage complementary and compensatory work.

Remember all relationships are actually between individual people who represent organisations. People skills are the key to developing relationships.

Building a power base

Organisations can link together to form a political or power base to argue from a common position.

> *The community association and the youth centre always back each other up on resources and issues...Neither of us gets much, but it's much better we don't spend our time fighting each other. We fight for the whole estate. We're much more likely to get heard too.*

> *When it comes to it, all the voluntary groups and the local authority people come together and present a solid face...We all work with young people after all. United we stand, divided we'd get picked off...*

There will be times when you need a political power base of people and organisations who share a common interest in the development and well-being of young people. Such organisations can come together as an action group. There may be a permanent organisation that supports young people in your area such as a:

- youth forum
- youth council
- worker's forum
- community forum

If there is, consider joining one. This may seem unnecessary. However, if young people are to be empowered, both they and you need to have opportunities to work in a political way. How can we teach young people about power and how it works in their local community if we let others determine our future?

> *I was thinking recently about all that stuff we did about political education on my youth work course in the early 1980s. What's happened to it all? There aren't any alliances anymore: only a voice for young people who conform. I'm sure that's what all this citizenship stuff is about. Political education has been stolen from us and they've replaced it with some woolly rubbish. No-one even fought to keep it, that's the really sad thing.* (Older part-time worker)

Being part of a power base has a number of advantages. It:

- Gives the youth worker and the young people a voice in a wider arena.
- Can assist in funding applications.
- Provides access to groups where otherwise young people and youth workers would not be represented.
- Offers an arena for young people to see and practice politics. Political education should be part of the youth work curriculum.
- Can provide better services for young people.
- Can be viewed as a form of investment of your time. It takes place on behalf of the workers and young people with whom you work.

Organisations sometimes have formal links with each other that are helpful in the delivery of the work. For example, the youth workers may refer homeless young people to a nearby foyer. As the relationship grows and trust between the two organisations develops, then the foyer may ask the youth workers to assist them with individual young people. The effect is to allow relationships that have already been built to be extended and make the young people feel more secure at a difficult time, as arrangements can be made smoothly.

These linkages are also helpful for workers, as they ease workloads and provide support and continuity. Highlighting the advantages and outcomes of such links can also prove useful in establishing the need to maintain and expand sectors of the service. Supportive relationships may develop between youth workers and sports clubs, between health workers and pastoral care staff at a school.

Each organisation and project has its own role. No one has the monopoly on truth and skill. Only when organisations respect each other and value the contributions that they each make, can young people get the full benefit from all the services on offer. The wider and more differentiated the ranges of opportunities are, the greater the range of young people who can get their needs met. Highly differentiated services allow young people to move from organisation to organisation, as their needs change.

Compensatory relationships

These are when one agency partner compensates for a gap in the range of opportunities offered by the other agency:

> The Police asked us to run young people's discos in the town when the professional DJ pulled out because of the constant feuding between two groups. Our purpose was to get the young people to be able to co-operate enough to use the town centre facilities at the same time, and also to get the disco reinstated. Well we did it for about five months, working with the groups to run the discos. Then we withdrew as we weren't needed anymore. The message had got through. The young people were well pleased, so were the Police.

> We don't try to offer counselling: there is a counselling agency that is excellent and accessible. We refer young people there and support them until they feel comfortable.

> The school only runs football teams for top players. Lots of the rural kids would like a game but can't get into the school team and the villages don't run junior teams or girl's teams. We don't run it really: the young people do...I suppose it's not cutting edge youth work but it meets a need and its fun and the young people take responsibility. It means we keep contact with groups of young people we otherwise wouldn't see.

Networks and youth work

These are a loose set of relationships which people enter into voluntarily. They offer its participants:

- sources of information
- ideas
- support
- help in difficult times
- practical help
- examples of good practice
- contact, they help to counter isolation

Participants in networks usually hold common values and concerns for young people: 'you are never alone in a network'.

Remember that unused networks dry up, so keep using them. Be aware that networks depend on everyone both giving and taking. Reciprocal arrangements are necessary, otherwise people feel used and leave the network, so give and take in equal measure!

In summary

Manage your boundaries effectively and the time that you invest in this should help you to be:

- In control of your work and more planned.
- More effective in that work.
- More supported and less stressed.

and have more time to do the job of working with young people.

If you succeed in achieving this, then you will have gone a considerable way to making yourself 'kipper proof!'

Chapter Fourteen

Time Management

Time hath, my lord, a wallet at its back...   (William Shakespeare)

This, presumably, was one of the earlier comments on value for money and cost effectiveness!

There are enormous pressures on youth workers' time.

> *Whatever you do, however hard you work, there's always a stream of young people wanting a piece of you. The trouble is, once you can see needs, you can't pretend they're not there. It's not just the young people making demands who take up the time. It's the staff team, parents...and it's the kids who don't come near you...who you ought to reach out to. It's endless.*

Then on top of all this, there are:

- reports and returns
- evaluating the work and its quality assurance systems
- 'doing' the money
- building and maintenance
- planning ahead and action plans
- staff meetings and training
- recruitment and support to workers
- publicity
- unexpected extras

> *I'm always being asked to comment on draft policies.*

> *They [the managers] think that I've nothing better to do than attend meetings for them.*

The only way to handle difficult situations successfully, with all these competing pressures, is to plan systematically. The alternative is to go into work and hit the ground running, fielding things as they hit you, and hoping you get the vital bits done before you go home exhausted. You do have a choice, and this book is taking the planned approach. Time is a resource and like any resource, it must be managed.

Start to plan your use of time now: don't put it off. The sooner that you start the sooner things will improve!

Here are four **tools** to help you use your **time** effectively and efficiently:

1. An overview of your time use in the coming year.
2. Being clear about the purpose of your work. See also Chapter 8 on Forward Planning.
3. Setting priorities.
4. Time lines.

An Overview of Your Time Use in the Coming Year

In order to manage your time you must first discover how you use your time. To do this you begin by researching and working out three sets of facts about the time you spend in work and how you use that time. You should record:

1. The number of **hours** that you are contracted to work for the organisation (paid or voluntary per week, per month or per year)
2. The **tasks** in your job and the number of **hours** that you spend on each task per week or per year
3. The number of **hours** (if any) you are prepared and able to work over and **above your contract**.

For some people, youth work is a job **and** a hobby. Others may wish simply to work their contracted hours. Leaving aside the arguments as to whether it is ethical, sensible or healthy to work a large amount of unpaid overtime, it is worth noting that youth workers tend to work until the job is done. As youth workers want to help young people grow and develop, so they are unlikely to walk away when a young person needs help. Accept that you will inevitably work unpaid overtime and build it into your planning, if this is the case. You may then be able to take time off in lieu (TOIL) if your organisation allows for such practices.

It is however, essential that you control this extra working, otherwise one day you will find that you do work unpaid overtime and end up resenting every minute of it. This is stressful, and will demotivate you and turn you off youth work. Make your decision about unpaid overtime, and stick to it. If the volume of this work feels a burden, review your decision and make changes.

When you have worked out these figures and recorded them, you are in a position to calculate your time use for the coming year.

The dart board method

People who have used this method to plan their work (so called because you subtract time as you would do scores on a dartboard!) have found that it worked. It may seem difficult at first, but is actually quite easy. In order to help you to try this method here is:

- a set of instructions
- a worked example
- a form with space for you to work out your own time use

Instructions for working out your time use

1. Write down the number of hours or sessions you are contracted to work per year: = **(a)**.
2. Subtract from this the time or sessions that you are required to work when the content is not in your professional control:
   - supervision meetings   • team meetings

- conferences
- writing annual reports
- training events (paid)

the total of these: = **(b)**

3. Now subtract **(b)** from **(a)**, to leave **(c)**.
4. Work out what ten per cent of **(c)** is: this ten per cent **(d)** is called the **noise level**. Noise level is the time wasted by interruptions, unexpected happenings and problems, and it needs to be taken into account.
5. Subtract the noise level **(d)** from **(c)**, to leave **(e)**. This figure **(e)** is the time you have left to do the key tasks of the job.
6. To deal with the key tasks, choose your first key task, record how many hours it will take per year and subtract it from the number of hours you have left **(e)**. Decide on the next task and repeat the process. Keep going until you get to **zero time**. **That's it!** You cannot add any more tasks, unless you delete some that you have already included.

A worked example

This is for a full-time worker managing a large centre based project.

Activity	Time taken up	No. of sessions remaining
Total number of sessions per year 10 x 45 weeks	450	450
Less time required for: • supervision • team meetings: • training: • writing annual plan and full time worker reports: sub total:	10 sessions 10 sessions 6 sessions 6 sessions .... 32 sessions	 418
noise level: 42 sessions		376
Key Task 1: To manage the centre		
• Staffing project: 3 sessions per week, 40 weeks per annum (3 x 40) • Admin, publicity and planning: (1 x 40) • Pre-sessional work and evaluation. (1 x 40) • Team meetings: • Staff supervision, plus appointments, induction etc. (1 x 40) • Steering group meetings	120 40 sessions 40 sessions 8 sessions 40 sessions 4 sessions	

● Reports for steering group meetings	4 sessions	
sub total:	256 sessions	120

Key Task 2: To assist with in-house training courses

● Part-time worker's Level One course:	25 sessions	
● Preparation for above:	5 sessions	
sub total:	30 sessions	90

Key Task 3: To develop the Area Youth Forum

● Monthly meeting with group:	12 sessions	
● Admin., publicity, etc.:	8 sessions	
● Residential event:	12 sessions	
● Preparation, evaluation for events:	8 sessions	
sub total:	40 sessions	50

Key Task 4: To develop links with the local school

● Deliver PHSE classes (1 x 20)	20 sessions	
● Preparation and evaluation for above:	10 sessions	
● Meetings with school:	8 sessions	
sub total:	38 sessions	12

Key Task 5: To represent the service on the Child Protection Committee

● Attending bimonthly meetings:	12 sessions	0000
● Seeking and disseminating information	4 sessions	deficit time!

Deficit time means
- There is insufficient time in the schedule for Key Task 5.
- Do not take on any more work without dropping something else.

Now put your figures in here

Activity	No. of sessions taken up	No. of sessions remaining
Total number of sessions/hours that you are contracted to work per year (a)		
Less time and frequency required for: (b)		
• supervision	sessions	
• team meetings	sessions	
• training	sessions	
• writing annual and full-time worker reports	sessions	
sub total:	sessions	(c)
(d) noise level (10% of (c))	sessions	(e)
(f) *Key Task 1:*		
• ————————————	sessions	
• ————————————	sessions	
• ————————————	sessions	
• ————————————	sessions	
sub-total ————————————	sessions	(g)
(h) *Key Task 2:*		
• ————————————	sessions	
• ————————————	sessions	
• ————————————	sessions	
• ————————————	sessions	
sub-total ————————————	sessions	(i)

(j) *Key Task 3:*

• _____	sessions	
• _____	sessions	
• _____	sessions	
• _____	sessions	
• _____	sessions	
sub-total: _____	sessions	(k)

(l) *Key Task 4:*

• _____	sessions	
• _____	sessions	
• _____	sessions	
• _____	sessions	
sub-total: _____	sessions	(m)

Continue subtracting your key tasks until zero is reached. You should not take on any more work after zero, unless you drop one of the key tasks or reduce its size. The exception to this rule is **Jam**.

Jam

Jam is a simple idea. Most youth workers come into youth work with things that they enjoyed doing and hoped that some young people would enjoy them too. It might have been:

- art and craft
- outdoor education
- local politics
- foreign travel
- drama
- conservation issues
- developing world issues

It is important that you get the opportunity to do things that you enjoy doing with young people. It will be one of the things that gives you a buzz, and that is an important stress-buster. It also helps keep you grounded and in touch with young people's issues. Bread keeps you alive; jam makes it interesting.

Everyone needs regular doses of jam to prevent them from becoming stale. This is why it might be a good idea to work on that special project or agree to take a group to Germany, even though you cannot quite make the time within your committed hours. In the end, the decision is yours alone.

Being Clear About the Purpose of Your Work

This yearly approach to time management is crucial for establishing a realistic working pattern. It should help to prevent you becoming overloaded. However, in the short term, on a day-to-day basis, different strategies are needed.

You need to be clear exactly what you are planning to do. Time management is dependent on a good planning process. This means that you should be able to state an aim, objectives to meet that aim and tasks to reach those objectives. Once these tasks are known, they can be allocated to individuals. The individual will then need to make decisions about what to do first.

Setting Priorities

There is a simple way to work out the order of competing tasks.

It is always worth spending ten or fifteen minutes at the beginning of the day having a cup of tea or coffee and a quiet think. This gives you the opportunity to work out what you need to achieve by the end of the day, but to do this, it is necessary to prioritise your work.

Divide your work into things that are:

- urgent and important
- urgent but not very important
- important but not very urgent
- neither urgent nor important

This will tell you what your priorities should be. Start with those things that are both urgent and important, and then work on the things that are urgent, but not so important, and so on, down the list.

Never put things off because they are difficult or boring. A job needs doing, when it needs doing and it will not go away. If you need help or support to do that piece of work, then try to find the support through your support network, see Chapter 15.

Case Study: Andy's task avoidance

Task avoidance is a way of putting things off, whilst seeming to work very hard. **Andy** knew that he must sort out a difficult matter with his manager. Quite suddenly, it is just the right moment to sort out the filing and find out about hiring a coach. Then he needed to go to the Community Association to make some arrangements for the Family Fun Day. By the end of the day, a number of tasks that were important were done. However, the task that was urgent and important still remained: talking to his manager about an awkward issue. He also continued to be constantly aware that he needed to see his manager, which was in itself stressful.

Andy phoned his friend Mac. They met after work and talked over the problem, developing a way of handling the meeting. Mac played the manager, until Andy felt more confident that he could cope. Then with Mac still there, Andy phoned his manager and left a message on the voice mail to fix a meeting. On the day of the meeting, Mac had a coffee with Andy and accompanied him as far as

the meeting. He contacted Andy after the meeting and 'debriefed' him. The outcomes were not as bad as he had feared; nor as good as he had hoped.
  If you know that you are avoiding a difficult task:

- Get support.
- Develop a plan and a time scale.
- Keep using the support and put your plan into action.

Time Lines

Some major tasks need small amounts of work done on them over a long period. Work needs to be done in a sequence. A time line is useful for keeping the planning on course. The time line needs to be produced before any work starts.

Case Study: Setting up a youth forum in the centre.

7–14 Sept.	All staff to talk with young people in the centre about the importance of getting their voice heard.
14 Sept.	Posters week
28 Sept.	Short meeting for anyone interested in Youth Forum. Propose an awayday to explore the idea in more detail. The day should include some training as well as team building and fun.
28 Sept–20 Oct.	Young people who have attended the meeting to invite other young people to come to awayday.
20 Oct	Awayday.
6–13 Nov.	Visits to other area's youth forums.
25 Nov.	Discussion about how the youth forum will work and ground rules, setting of first agenda.
10 Dec.	First Youth Forum meeting.

A Final Thought

Many people put themselves under pressure of time by their own actions. Here is a list of things to which the authors plead guilty, from time to time:

- Putting off difficult jobs.
- Not delegating.
- Getting dates muddled.
- Spending time on things that we find enjoyable.
- Chatting on the phone.
- Not planning our day, nor setting priorities.

  Look at your time use honestly. Make changes and get it under control. Once your boundary and time management is under control your stress level should reduce.

Chapter Fifteen

Stress

It is essential to understand what **stress** is and what happens inside the body when levels of stress rise. Biologically, humans are highly evolved animals, who still retain the mechanisms to survive in the wild: the instinct to hunt, find food, escape from danger or fight it. However skilled people become at 'consultation', being 'assertive rather than aggressive', and 'recognising feelings', the human body is still out there in the wild, surviving.

Fight or Flight

When threatened, animals and humans need to either fight or flee. The autonomic nervous system reacts instantly and gears the body up to do one or the other, by increasing the adrenaline in the blood. This in turn increases the basic body rate, the heart pumps faster, blood pressure rises as does the sweat rate. Sugar is released into the blood stream becoming available for instant energy. At the same time the digestive process slows as does salivation and the flow of blood through the skin and gut. This is why your mouth goes dry. Physically then you are ready for anything.

Once the threat is past, the parasympathetic nervous system assists us to rest and recover. It increases digestion and gut mobility, and causes the sugar to go back into store. It decreases the heart rate and blood pressure.

When we are stressed we go into **fight or flight** mode, so it follows that to manage stress we need to encourage our parasympathetic nervous system to help us rest and recover. If we stay in fight or flight mode for too long, our body becomes damaged. We are not always good at recognising our stress levels.

Selye has developed a model, see Figure 11, that explains how different levels of stress are linked to feelings, and suggests that there are four basic stress states:

1. hypostress
2. hyperstress
3. distress
4. eustress

Hypostress

When we are under-stressed we become bored, fed up and restless. This is in itself stressful.

> I go down to the beach and have a swim, then I think how good it would be to relax. For the first ten minutes it's great. Then I notice a fly buzzing near me, and sand gets into places it shouldn't. Then I start to wriggle and five minutes later I'm walking along the shoreline. I hate relaxing.

Figure 11: Selye's model of stages of stress

Eustress

Feeling confident, focused, ready to go but comfortable.

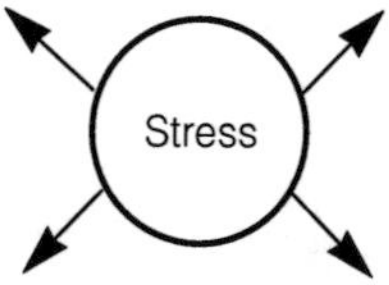

Hyperstress

Becoming ineffective as the result of stress

No longer on an even keel

Mood swings with sudden bursts of anger.

Stress

Hypostress

Too little stress = boredom

Distress

The stress has affected the body to the point that it is sick:
- ulcers
- insomnia
- headaches
- high blood pressure
- heart attacks
- death

I loathe evenings when there are no young people about: it makes me uptight.

This is **hypostress**. Most people cannot totally shut down their body from the fight or flight mode without learning to relax.

Hyperstress

Hyperstress impairs our ability to think and function effectively. This is the state that most people describe as 'feeling stressed'.

I went to bed late because I had to finish the report and slept through my alarm. When I woke up I didn't feel rested. Then I realised I was meant to be at the meeting to present the report, so I got showered, dressed and out of the flat in less than ten minutes. I jumped into the car and then remembered I'd left the report in the sitting room so I raced back to get it. Somehow, I must have put my keys down. I knew what I had done when I heard the front door click. I was locked out and my car keys were inside. I ran back to the car to find it locked with my phone inside. It took me an hour to sort it all out and I missed the bloody meeting completely.

This worker was so 'wound up' that she was not able to think clearly about simple routine matters.

Distress

Distress is when the stress is so extreme and unrelenting that our bodies and minds begin to suffer. It can lead to seriously high blood pressure, ulcers and heart problems: sufferers become subject to an increased risk of heart attack and strokes. When stress affects the mind the result can be 'burnout' and depression.

If we use 'props' to help us cope with the stress, they can cause problems: alcohol, cigarettes, comfort eating, and pills in excess, all result in health problems.

Eustress

This is the perfect state of tension to ensure the body works effectively and efficiently. There is enough tension to make the person feel confident and relaxed, but not enough to make them ineffective. The feeling is 'It's OK—I can handle it.' The person is totally focused. To see this in action, look at a high jumper just before he or she begins their run, or a conductor of an orchestra just before they begin a performance.

Eustress is achieved by controlling the fight or flight responses, so they work **for** you, instead of **against** you. There are a number of steps you can take, to help you achieve this:

1. Find someone to talk to

Find an individual or a group that you feel able to talk to in an open and honest way. This should help you to:
* Share feelings, and get difficulties in proportion and keep them there.
* Find strategies to reduce stress levels.
* Focus on achievements (think positive).
Or find a non-hierarchical supervisor whom you can trust.
Try not to have a 'isn't life awful' session. This will only serve to trap you where you are.

2. Look after your health

Eat healthily: remember that the effect of stress (fight or flight) is to cause sugar to be dumped into your blood stream and your blood pressure to rise. Do not add to the problem by carrying out youth work on a diet of strong coffee, donuts, chocolate bars, cheese sandwiches and crisps. All of these foods act to push up your blood pressure.

Tea and coffee contain caffeine. Donuts and chocolate bars contain high quantities of fat and sugar; cheese sandwiches are full of fat and salt. There is nothing wrong with any of these foods in small quantities but as a regular diet they are extremely unhealthy. Youth workers often work combinations of hours that make it difficult to eat well. Many have access to sweets and fast foods: it's easy to snack your way through the day.

3. Take exercise

If you are having a stressful time go for a slow steady walk: it will help your body to shift from fight or flight to normal. Fresh air should clear your head, make you feel better and make you more effective. Going for a run will only put up your blood pressure and put the body back in stressed mode.

If you really can't get away and you are feeling very stressed, try four or five slow deep breaths. Make sure your ribs are spread out and that you don't raise your shoulders. Closing your eyes may help. The exercise should relax you and the achievement of a little piece of personal space will help to keep you focused.

If you are regularly very stressed you might consider taking up an activity that decreases stress, such as yoga, tai chi or meditation, and making this part of your daily routine.

4. Take your holidays and time off in lieu (TOIL)

Too many youth workers say things like:

> I can't fit in my leave. There is so much to do and if I don't do it there's no one around who will do it. It's the young people who lose out at the end of the day.

You cannot work 24 hours a day for 365 days of the year. Even if you could, there would still be young people around whom you would not be able to help. Working way over the time you are contracted to do, or taking on too many part-time contracts may be tempting but sooner or later you will burnout or be ill. If your employer really wants the work done then they must find someone else to do it.

5. Make sure you have a life other than youth work

Have friends who do other things. It is very easy to slip into only mixing with youth workers; for one thing, the unsociable hours mean that people who do other things are not necessarily around when we are free.

Youth workers often work in teams who:

- Face common difficulties.
- Plan and work together to help young people grow and develop.
- Monitor and evaluate young people's development together.
- Share feelings, problems, successes and failures, and support each other.

This gives teams a 'family feel' and it is easy to be sucked into these relationships and not be able to see past them. Part-time workers are often better off in this respect as they usually have more links outside of youth work.

Whatever your situation find something that you enjoy and find relaxing, whether it's music or model railways. Make sure that you engage in the activity that you enjoy on a regular basis.

Sit down and work out what are the most stressful things that you do and why they are stressful: find a friend who can help with this.

Use this plan to rearrange your work, and your personal life so that:

- Not too many stressful things happen on the same day: spread these throughout the week or month.
- Wherever possible, a stressful activity is followed by a less stressful one or a stress buster.
- Every day contains something that you really enjoy.

Next take a look at the stress points and see if they have anything in common. If there are common causes, then you need to deal with these. Use your support framework set out in Chapter 15 to find a starting point.

If you are:

- Extremely stressed and feeling unable to cope.
- Depressed to a point where you struggle to cope.
- Coping with stress by using props to excess.
- Feeling ill with something that doesn't clear up.

you need to see a doctor or possibly even a good counsellor. There is a point where self-help is not sufficient.

Chapter Sixteen

Support Frameworks

What is a Support Framework?

Support means different things to different people. Support may be:

> *...Having someone there for you: they don't have to agree with you, just care that you are OK.*

> *...Being with someone who can take me out of myself...It helps me see the world differently when I am locked into a problem. My friends can make me laugh, stand the whole thing on its head and I can see a way forward.*

> *I know this is going to sound daft but it's books...if I have a problem I use a book to give me ideas. If I want to escape from the world, I read a book. If I want to get creative, I read poetry...I guess I must be on my own here, people sometimes make things worse.*

> *...A range of people, I go to different people for different things. I go to Carol if I hurt and I want comfort, and to Ian for ideas. I go to Jo if I want to stand back and take a long hard look at what has happened and how to move forward.*

Research has shown that workers identified six different types of support:

1. A place to go

This will be somewhere to go and be accepted, where you will be physically cared for and no pressure will be put on you.

2. Someone who will help you review your work systematically

This will be someone who listens to you, helps you learn from your experience and supports you to make decisions. This may happen formally in management supervision, or in non-line management supervision. Alternatively, you may have a friend or colleague to help you. They need not necessarily be a youth worker, just a good listener with an analytical mind who you trust and find helpful.

3. An ideas person or group

This can be an exciting process that is highly motivating, and often amusing, as people go over the top with ideas. It may be characterised by phrases like:

> *Why don't we...*
> *What if...*

...yeah and we could...
...And then...

4. A problem solver

This is a person who can focus on an issue, draw out the strands, identifying the real problem and then helping you to solve it. The role is rather like a 'systematic review'. It might be the same person but you do need a high level of trust here because the problem that you present may not be the actual problem.

Case Study: Oz

Oz had been a youth worker for eight years in an Arts and Drama team. He loved the work and was totally absorbed by it. The Arts team was close, he was well liked and had many friends in the group. One day he said he was having trouble with the improvised play he was doing. It just wouldn't go right. Three weeks later he was in despair.

The team leader suggested people who could work with him. Oz refused help. The team leader suggested people outside the team who might assist. Oz rejected that idea too, and went off sick. The person he talked to was an old friend from his college days called Lou. Oz's real problem was that he had met someone that he wanted to live with and that meant moving away from the area and leaving the job. He couldn't face telling the group that he was going to leave. He felt that he had let them down and was somehow betraying their trust. Lou helped him to identify the problem, and to tell the team about his plans. In reality, the group were delighted for him, and he is still in contact with them. He and his partner attend events that the team put on from time to time.

Not all problems are big, or potentially life changing, but many work problems do link to private lives. Conversely, many problems with our private lives also have an effect upon our work.

5. A group of 'people like you'

Depending on who you are, these might be:
- detached workers
- workers in charge of projects
- gay, lesbian or bisexual workers
- women managers
- black worker's groups
- trainees on the part-time youth work course

The group provides you with opportunities to share experiences, get information and listen to others who have handled difficulties that you might also be having. The group is empathetic. They know how you feel because they have been there, and this lessens any feelings of isolation.

6. Outside sources of information

This might include:

- your Union
- going to conferences
- regional meetings
- Youth work organisations such as the National Youth Agency, Youth Clubs UK, etc. There are many, many more.

These organisations introduce you to new ideas, and provide information, and help, but they are not part of your immediate work environment and therefore not limited by it. Work communities tend to become limited and entrapping. People see things in similar ways, so they might do things as they have always done because:

> *We always do it this way.*
> *It's easier not to make waves.*

Outside bodies are stimulating and help you escape from the limitations of your own organisation.

How to Form a Support Framework

1. Find a person or organisation who can offer support in each of these six areas.
2. Contact the people you have identified and explain that you would like them to be part of your support network and gain their agreement for the role that you are asking them to play.
3. Set the ground rules together. Ask the questions:
   - Is this a reciprocal arrangement?
   - Do they want you to be part of their support framework? If so, what is your role in relation to them?
   - Are there times when they do not wish to be contacted? There may be times when contact would be intrusive. Make sure they know that they must tell you if you are overloading them, and that you would ask them to do this, so you can maintain the relationship.

When forming your support framework remember that your manager's role should be restricted to that of a systematic reviewer, and an ideas person, if they have the skills. Managers may be problem solvers if the relationship is right but they should never be 'a place to go' as this compromises the managerial relationship.

No single person can fulfil more than two of the framework slots. If you rely on too few people the effect will be to overload them, and you will be without support, if they move away. Further, your framework will lack a width of ideas and information. Using a partner or parent can also put a strain on that relationship.

People seldom need all six areas of support at once: depending on their situation, people have different needs. For instance, if starting a new job, the person might need:

- a place to go
- people like you
- systematic review

Someone with a major problem at work may use:

- a place to go
- problem solvers
- ideas people
- outside sources of information

If you feel that you are getting stale it might be wise to have:

- systematic review
- outside sources of information
- ideas people

If you are just jogging along, these may serve your purpose:

- systematic review
- ideas people
- people like you
- outside sources of information

What Are Your Roles if You Manage People?

As a manager your responsibility is to use a line management session to explain to them what a support framework is and check out that they have a framework in place, or are starting to build one.

This is delicate work, because you have no right to ask who these people are; it is not your business unless they choose to tell you. All you need to do is to ensure that they have a network in place. If you are asked you can make suggestions of people that they might contact to complete that framework.

You should also discuss with all those you supervise what they see as your support role and their expectations of you. You need to consider their expectations carefully and only agree to a role that is realistic, bearing in mind your work load and skills. This arrangement will need reviewing from time to time to see how it is working. Following this review, appropriate adjustments can be made.

Remember that nothing can remove your responsibility to help those you manage:

- review their work systematically
- learn from the process
- develop plans from the outcomes of this work review

If your manager hasn't asked about your support framework and their role in it you may have to take the initiative. To help you do this, here is a framework you can photocopy:

Support framework	
Role	People
1. Somewhere to go and be accepted. 2. Systematic review of action. 3. Creative thinking. 4. Problem solving. 5. People like me. 6. Outside information.	

Saying 'No'!

If you are a good worker, everyone wants a piece of you. Someone once said that youth workers have to be all things to all people. Young people, managers, parents, other agencies, all want your time and effort. If you say yes to all their requests it will stretch your boundaries, and over-load your time, and you! Some of the people who want your time will be open and honest:

> *Could you give us a hand at the fete? We've some young people who want to do a stall and we haven't got anyone who feels they can work with them: they're very lively!*   (Church-based voluntary organisation)

This straightforward approach leaves you with a number of options:

> *Yes* or *I'm sorry I just don't have the time* or *Well, I could just do (specify time or other limits)...*

However, many people put an emotional twist on their request that makes it much harder just to say 'no'. To say 'no' you need to be assertive. Requests may come in packages like this:

> *...And if you don't then the kids will miss out again, so I hope you can do it.*

This may be true, but it is not a reason to put yourself under pressure. Someone has identified a need that they cannot meet. Do not allow your 'I feel guilty if I don't give all of me' button to be pressed. Analyse the situation:

- How much time and effort will it take?
- What is the likelihood of the young people getting significant learning from the situation?
- Will you learn from the process?
- Is there any other reason for saying yes: do you owe the asker a favour? Do you wish to develop a positive relationship with the individual, or the organisation?

You cannot answer these questions in an instant, so make yourself time by replying:

> *I'm not sure if I've got time so I will get back to you tomorrow.*

When you have decided on your reply, make it clearly and professionally without bad temper, apologies or long explanations.

> *I'm sorry I can't help you, I haven't got time. If you give me more notice another time, we might be able to arrange something in the future.*

This reply will both protect your boundary, and maintain a relationship with the asker.

Other ways of coercing you into work that you would not otherwise do, include a mixture of desperation and flattery:

> *I wouldn't normally ask, I know how busy you are but I'm desperate and you are the best person for the job: you could hit the ground running.*

I'm in a real mess, I know it's nothing to do with you but can you just give me a hand to...

Whatever the situation:

- Make yourself time and space.
- Do the analysis.
- Make your decision, whether it should be 'no' or 'yes' and decide on any conditions upon which you will say yes.
- Give your reply assertively.

Assertiveness requires you to make good eye contact, be relaxed but keep your body still, and evenly balanced:

- Be open and honest.
- Acknowledge the other person's situation.
- Explain your position.
- Give your answer.

For example:

Yes I would like to be a tutor, what happens now?

or

I realise how important youth work training is, and that you are a tutor short. From past experience I know it takes about 25 sessions to tutor on the introductory course. I just do not have two and a half weeks to spare before Christmas.

or

I realise how important youth work training is, and I would like to be a tutor again. I know from past experience that it takes about 25 sessions to tutor on the introductory course. I can only do it if I cut down the youth work activities and delay setting up the Helpline until the New Year.

If further pressure is put on you, try the 'broken record' technique. Reply:

I understand that but as I have said...

Do not become drawn into discussion when you have already made your decision. It is not helpful to say:

Which part of 'no' don't you understand?

Chapter Seventeen

What Makes a Good Manager?

One of the hardest transitions to make, is from being responsible for yourself and your work, to being responsible for the work of others: that of becoming a **manager**. Youth workers often find it hard to become managers because:

- The management that they have received may have been poor, i.e. authoritarian and inflexible, or weak and ineffective. They reject the styles but do not have another model on which to draw.
- It is sometimes scary to be responsible for other people and their work.
- They see **power** as a negative force, that can be abused, and may result in people being damaged.

These feelings are often helped by exploring the nature of power, and how it can be used positively.

Abuse of power	Positive use of power
Using power to serve your own ends. Bullying and coercion. Limiting others' potential. Taking credit for others' achievements. Suppressing information that should . be public Letting power hang: failing to act when action is needed	Preventing discrimination. Helping others to develop. Providing opportunities for individuals and teams. Encouraging creativity and new ideas. Accepting the risks so that others can try out new ideas. Being brave and proactive.

What is Power?

One definition is:

The ability to direct other people towards an outcome.

There are many different types of personal power.

Positional power

Police officers, managers, youth workers, all have power because of their positions. Police officers have power by Act of Parliament. Managers have positional power vested in them by their contract and job description.

Expert power

This is power you have because others recognise your skills, abilities and experience. This gives you influence.

Charismatic power

This is a subtle mix of communication skills, energy, and sense of personal direction and commitment; it attracts people. Hitler, Thatcher and Princess Diana all had charismatic power.

Coercive power

This is the ability to force people to do what you want. For example, if a teacher or lecturer is going to mark your essay, then they have coercive power over you to reflect their views back to them. If someone has the power to give, or withhold, something from you, then whether they recognise it or not, they have coercive power over you.

Resource power

This stems from having the ability to give others' material things, or the use of material things. The expression 'taking your bat and ball home' acknowledges this, as does the term 'purchasing power.' If you hold resources then you will find that people come around you.

Paper power

Qualifications can provide access. A driving license gives you permission to drive, a weight training instructor's certificate gives you permission to train others, and a degree gives you access to certain jobs.

Knowledge is power

It is not just what you know, but whom you know, that gives you power. It gives you entry into groups of people who all in turn share information with each other, for example, sub-groups in political parties, pressure groups and networks. In the same way partners, children and friends of people who are powerful take on a power of their own. If the child of the Chair of the County Council Education Committee comes to your youth project, then you have the potential to influence the Chair's power.

It is important to know whether and what kind of power you have: you can then increase it if you wish. Try this exercise to begin to understand your power. Work with a friend to get an insight into your power. Be honest, do not deny the power that you hold. Fill in the table, and then think about how, and why, you would like to change the situation.

What power do you have and to whom does that relate?		
Type of power	Describe the power you have	Do you wish to decrease or increase this area of power and if so why?
• positional power • expert power • charismatic power • coercive power • resource power • paper power • knowing people with power		

Case Study: Expert power

'I found that my greatest potential power was 'expert power'. I've worked in the same youth club for 20 years, know all about the area and its resources for young people. The club has helped literally thousands of young people. All the services, social services, police, schools etc. phone me when it suits them but no one recognised me. I was just the part-time worker in charge of the youth club who lived on the estate. I've not got any real qualifications except the part-time youth worker's qualification...

...well, I worked out a strategy for making my expert power work for the estate and the young people.

I turned up at the professional workers' lunch. When it came to the meeting, people started talking rubbish, so I told them what really happens. They were amazed. None of them really knew the estate...and I became an expert.

They asked me onto a planning group, to apply for funding. I got some of the women who had been youth club members into the group, then the youth club forum was asked... It's no good knowing stuff if people don't know you know it! This all gave the club *knowledge power* and even some *resource power*.

I found that I got *too much* power. Everyone was leaving it all to me to make decisions, and to organise everyone... So I started to delegate more and offer support at the same time... Then we all grew.

In supervision and at the team meeting, we choose pairs. Every pair agreed to do a project, and take full responsibility for it... They weren't all brilliant, but we reviewed them all and I gave lots of positive feedback. It changed the pattern.

After I'd done all this I realised my boss only had *positional power* and *knowledge power*. I had more than him in all the other slots...so I switched how I approached him. I didn't argue, I was the expert and charismatic. Being an expert gave me loads of confidence... It worked, now we don't row so much and I get a 'yes' more often.'

Developing a Management Style

How does a manager develop a style that encourages growth, and flexibility, and fun, while at the same time holding the unit together and ensuring that it meets its targets? The answer is with great difficulty!

There are three basic rules:

1. Motivation.
2. Being a model of good practice.
3. Offering constructive feedback.

1. Motivation

One way of looking at motivation is to consider what makes us feel good, and what has the opposite effect.

We feel good when we:

- Get positive recognition of our work and ourselves.
- Feel that our work is making a difference.
- Know that we are growing and developing.
- Resolve problems on our own.

Getting positive recognition of our work and ourselves

This can come from the 'put ups' discussed in Chapter 5, from the process of managerial supervision or in casual conversation. It is no good if the praise is false as people recognise this. False praise is de-motivating.

> *Our area officer comes round and inspects us about once a month. He's learned about the **praise sandwich**, so each time he leaves, he tells us:*
> - *One thing we are doing well.*
> - *One thing he wants us to stop, change, or do better.*
> - *One thing he thinks is good.*
> *Only he doesn't mean the first and the last bits, just the criticism in the middle.'*

So:

- Praise only counts fully, when it comes from someone you respect.
- Give praise honestly, or not at all.
- Create a way of working which is full of 'put ups'.

Feel that our work is making a difference.

No amount of praise for a job well done can motivate us if we 'thought the job was crap in the first place'. Youth work is a roller coaster of emotion, as the youth worker's success is tied up with that of the young people they work for; and therein lies the dilemma.

> *I feel uplifted when they succeed, and de-motivated when they get into difficulties yet again. My manager says that I need more emotional distance. She doesn't seem to understand that it is my work that contributes to their success: my sweat, my efforts, my emotions. How can you teach people to love without showing love? How can I*

show them love and have true emotional distance at the same time? I do step back and say to myself, 'it's only a job'. I know it is, but it's one that I care about a lot...

As a manager it is important to help people to separate their feeling of achievement from the achievements of the young people with whom they work. It's great if the work is good and the outcomes are successful for the young people. As managers, we need to recognise that this may not always be the case, and that the work may have been just as good, but not end in success for the young people. The young people themselves, and the workers, need to be able to cope with this to stay motivated. This is part of the growth process. We need to help people we manage to see the worth of their work, even, and especially, when the gains to young people are not immediately obvious.

Know that we are growing and developing

This occurs when we:
- Are given more responsibility through job development or promotion.
- Finish a course successfully.
- Succeed in doing things that we didn't know we could do, such as handling a crisis.

I know it was awful Angie getting hurt, but now its all over I'm really proud of myself: I didn't panic. I did all the right things; everyone stayed calm; we talked it through with the kids afterwards. Everyone learned a bit and I feel like superwoman...is that an awful thing to say?

Equally doing new activities can be as enjoyable for us, as for the young people.

I went on a residential with the youth orchestra. They needed an extra female staff member. I'm not musical, I've never played an instrument. Well...they taught me to play some percussion a bit, and I actually played in the orchestra...it was fantastic.

Resolve problems on our own

It is important to have support and help available, but not to have the job taken out of our hands while we stand by, this makes us feel useless, like a spare part. When that happens, every moment is agony. So ensure that you and all those whom you manage:
- Have achievable challenges, and celebrate the outcomes.
- Delegate, develop people's jobs: it 'grows' people.
- Never, where possible, take over another's work.
- Feel included, part of the team.

Feeling part of the team comes through a whole set of formal and informal activities. Having a personal coffee mug in the cupboard may be as important as having the minutes of the team meeting sent on time.

Teams need to be built and maintained and this is the job of the team leader or manager. An effective, professional team needs to have members who:
- Share a common vision for the work.

- Have a common language built up over time from the shared experiences of training and working together. This aids communication.
- Are cohesive.
- Support each other.
- Are open and honest with each other about the work and how they feel about it.
- Have confidence in each other, enough to work together effectively.
- Trust each other.
- Understand, and discuss, the unwritten rules of the group and the effect these are having on the group.
- Help newcomers to join the group and others to exit from it.

All this requires time and commitment from the team leader. There are five key tasks:

1. Establish and maintain a safe working climate.
2. Set aside time for the team to work out a common purpose. This can be done as part of the team-building process on awaydays or extended team meetings. This will need reaffirming or altering on occasions.
3. Ensure that everyone in the team gets opportunities to work with everyone.
4. Deal with conflicts before they fester and cause damage that cannot be repaired. This requires the courage to raise the matter, the ability to listen to all sides without making judgements and the skills to find a solution where no-one loses face. This means a **win-win** solution. Win-win solutions require compromise from everyone. Achieving this may mean meeting with individuals and sub-groups to unlock their thinking and allow them to move forward.
5. Keep the core of the team working; organise the information flow; identify current or potential issues and deal with them; offer support; deal with the outside world on behalf of the team; keep an overview of the work and keep it in balance.

2. Be a model of good practice

Make sure that the way **you** treat **your** team is a model of how you expect **them** to work with young people or a 'self demonstrating model of good practice.' It makes your unit consistent which means that there is a single message about:

- valuing people
- anti oppressive practice
- encouraging and valuing learning
- encouraging creativity and challenge

This is the 'do as I do, and do as I say' model!

3. Offer constructive feedback

In order to do this you need to understand feedback. Feedback is the way that each of us knows how the people we meet feel about and respond to the message, or signals we send them through:

- words
- body language
- writing

For instance, look at Carl and Linda, in Figure 12.

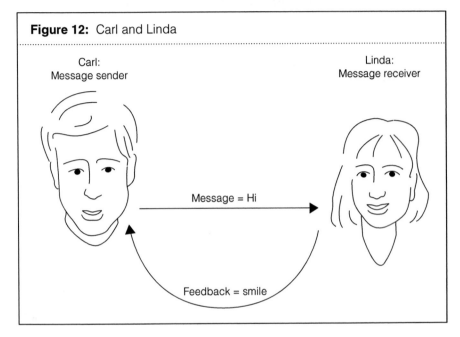

Figure 12: Carl and Linda

Carl:
Message sender

Linda:
Message receiver

Message = Hi

Feedback = smile

Carl, sender of message:	*Hi.*
Linda, receiver of message:	Smiles.
Carl:	*How are you?*
Linda:	*Great, I've just got a new job.*
Carl:	Looks fed up.
Linda:	*Aren't you pleased for me?*
Carl:	*Of course, but I've just lost mine.*
Linda:	*I'm so sorry, let me give you a hug.*
Carl:	Approaches with open arms.
Linda:	Opens her arms to hug him.

Carl's learning:	She likes and values me.
	She cares what happens to me.
	She is on my wave length.

Linda's learning:	He likes and values me.
	He's hurting.
	I can help him with the pain.

Giving and receiving feedback is not quite as simple as Figure 12 shows though as signals can be blocked or distorted, as in Figure 13.

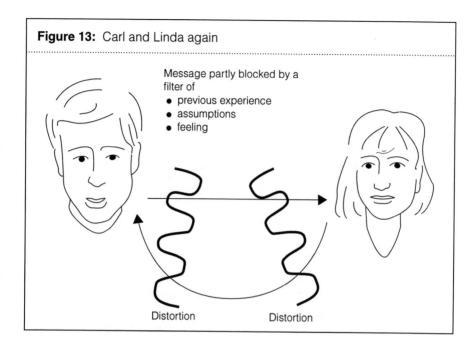

Figure 13: Carl and Linda again

Message partly blocked by a filter of
- previous experience
- assumptions
- feeling

Distortion   Distortion

If Carl or Linda's sensitivity to each other is blocked by their own feelings, then this might happen.

Linda speaking to a friend, after seeing Carl:

I saw Carl today, he was in a foul mood: I didn't stop to chat, I don't know what's the matter with him.

Or, Carl, speaking to his friend:

I bumped into Linda today. We never really chatted. I think I annoyed her.

In Figure 12 and the first part of the example, Carl and Linda were both good at reading signals so each had a positive outcome from their encounter. In Figure 13 and the second part of the example, feelings interfered with the communication and were never resolved.

Interference can also be caused by cultural factors. For example, a younger person making full eye contact with an older person may be seen as open and honest, or paradoxically, as exactly the opposite, disrespectful and cheeky. Interference can also be blocked by experience and people internalising the experience as 'the truth'. e.g."

- 'All men are just after sex.'
- 'Women who look like that lie a lot.'

Prejudices may alter the message or signal that we send or receive.

Feedback can be all sorts of things. Put ups and put downs are all pieces of feedback. Feedback can be very tiny pieces of body language, which can convey large messages. A wink meaning 'that's what I've said to them but you and I know different, don't we!' or a slight fleeting upturn of the mouth meaning 'I'm really, really happy but I don't want to show it now in this situation.' It needs practice and skill to read these signals accurately. Most youth workers are excellent at this.

The power of feedback

Feedback tells us how others see us, and is very powerful in the effect it has on people. In our heads we have two major ideas about ourselves:

- Self image: how we see ourselves.
- Self esteem: how we feel about what we see.

Feedback is absorbed immediately by the brain and affects self image and esteem: it is very powerful. It changes how people see themselves and how they feel about it. There are three types of feedback, positive and negative feedback, and constructive criticism.

Positive feedback or praise

> *Well done.*
> *I liked the way you involved so many young people.*
> *You must have worked hard to get that level of involvement in that space of time.*

Positive feedback makes you feel good, raises your self esteem and reinforces the value of things that you can already do, but you learn nothing else from it.

Negative feedback

> *That was a mess.*
> *If I couldn't do it better then I wouldn't have started.*
> *If you were the last person on earth I wouldn't ask you to do it...*

This offers no learning and damages the receiver's self image and esteem, and may destroy their confidence.

Constructive criticism

This occurs when feedback is offered in a way that helps the receiver to grow and develop. It opens doors through which the receiver may choose to walk. In order to do this the sender has to say negative things to the receiver in a way that they can hear, accept and want to deal with.

Case Study: Diane and Rod, manager and worker

Two young men, both aged 15 years, started to square up to one another, and began to throw punches. The rest of the members formed a ring and shouted 'fight, fight.' It all happened in a matter of seconds.

Rod, a part-time worker in training, pushed his way through the ring, grabbed the young men by their necks and hustled them out of the door. He shouted, 'Go home and don't come back until you can behave.'

Diane, the worker in charge, spent the next 15 minutes settling back down the group in the centre. She got everyone to sit in a circle and asked gently 'What happened?...How did you feel...Would you do the same again?'

Halfway through the process, Rod slipped away to the toilet, and then went outside. A young woman said 'I don't think Rod should have chucked them out like that' and the rest of the group agreed. Diane said: 'Let's have a break now: can someone make some tea or coffee please?'

She then went out to Rod. She greeted him with: 'Thank you for acting so quickly, no-one got hurt.'

He looked down and remained tense.

Diane said, 'No, I mean it Rod. You saw what was happening and sorted it quickly. The way you intervened was excellent.'

Rod said, 'But you heard what the kids were saying. They thought I was out of order throwing them out like that.'

Diane said '...so did I Rod. I said "the way you got in so quickly was great" and then you did what you thought was right, no one can do more than that. What I'd like to explore very quickly is what else you could have done, and what the young people would learn from the alternatives.'

Rod said, 'OK but what am I going to say to the kids?'

Diane said, 'Fine, I'll support you with that...'

Rod began to relax and immediately worked out that his alternatives were to:
- Try to sort out the problem on the floor: this would have been almost impossible.
- Ask the young men to come to the office to sort it out.

With prompting, he agreed that throwing the young men out taught the young people that physical strength wins if you are prepared to use it. However, the strategy of getting the young men into the office might have offered the group learning about resolving matters by negotiation, rather than by violence.

Rod said, 'Made a mess of it didn't I?'

Diane said, 'No, you did what you thought was the best at the time. You've thought about it and learned a bit about dealing with conflict.'

Rod said, 'So what do I say to the young people?'

Diane said, 'How about what I've just said. They'll understand: it happens to them all the time! You've done well.'

Rod said, light dawning in his eyes, '...yeah, thanks, will you get them together?'

Rod told the group about his new thoughts on how he should have acted. It worked. In ten minutes, Rod had learned a lot about:
- handling conflict
- reviewing work
- learning, as a basis of youth work

Diane had used the constructive criticism process to:
- praise
- criticise
- action plan
- reinforce the positive and the learning
- support the worker in putting the plan into action

Personal Style

Considering, and formulating, our own personal style is extremely difficult. We are so caught up with doing things that we often lose sight of ourselves in the process, so we genuinely do not know exactly what we did.

We can always ask the people for whom we work, for feedback about our personal style, though we may hesitate to do so for fear of:

- Hearing things we would rather were not said.
- Discovering that people knew something that we thought of as our secret.

If we are to expand and modify our personal style, we need to review it, and this means asking others how our style affects them. One way of doing this is to use a framework developed by Lesley Button. He started from the premise that there are lines on which our behaviour moves up or down: these are called continuums. For example, we move from passive through to being active through various points along a continuous line.

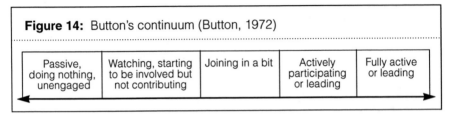

Figure 14: Button's continuum (Button, 1972)

| Passive, doing nothing, unengaged | Watching, starting to be involved but not contributing | Joining in a bit | Actively participating or leading | Fully active or leading |

He suggested that there are five similar lines on which all leaders and facilitators move and that it is possible to put a mark on each line to indicate where a facilitator or leader is at any given time. One example of this, is a worker encouraging a group to make a decision about how and when to do a mural on a neighbourhood wall, see Figure 15.

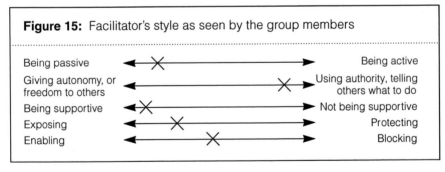

Figure 15: Facilitator's style as seen by the group members

Being passive — Being active
Giving autonomy, or freedom to others — Using authority, telling others what to do
Being supportive — Not being supportive
Exposing — Protecting
Enabling — Blocking

The style of the worker is quite laid back, encouraging the group to put forward their ideas and being generally helpful about how to put these into action. The facilitator is occasionally being quite **exposing** towards the group, by saying, 'let's go round the circle and everyone say what they think'. 'Barry, do you agree?' This keeps everyone involved, and exposes each person to contributing. The level of exposure for each person will depend on their willingness to contribute ideas.

A second example is the same worker trying to persuade a very drunk young man to accept a lift home. A group of the young man's friends are having a laugh about what is happening and are not helping the situation, see Figure 16.

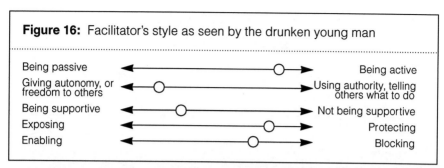

Figure 16: Facilitator's style as seen by the drunken young man

Being passive	Being active
Giving autonomy, or freedom to others	Using authority, telling others what to do
Being supportive	Not being supportive
Exposing	Protecting
Enabling	Blocking

The worker is keeping control of the situation but in order not to 'wind' anyone up, he is being soothing, **protective** and **supporting** to the drunk young man and his mates. He has decided that getting angry and authoritarian will only make matters worse. He is enabling in that he is encouraging the young man to get in the car and the crowd to move on. He is **blocking** in that he has put his body between the young man and the crowd. He speaks quietly in his ear in order to stop the crowd of friends urging the young man to show off, or do something stupid.

There is no right combination of positions on any continuum, only the ones that work for you, at the time, and in the situation that you find yourself. The most skilful facilitator or leader can:

- Work at all points of each line.
- Work on any combination of points on the five lines.
- Select the combination of points that will work best in a given situation.

The skills here are:
- sensitivity
- being able to read a situation
- flexibility.

A poor leader or facilitator is stuck in one style regardless of the situation. This inflexibility and insensitivity makes people feel unsafe. All of us have a preferred style that we slip into, this is how people remember our leadership style. One way of getting feedback on your style is to photocopy the five continuums and to ask each person that you manage or work with to put a mark on each line indicating what they see as your leadership style. Then ask people to hand them to back to you anonymously or, if they are willing to explain why they put the lines where they did, to talk to you about it. The information you gather should help you to review your style.

There are two other ways of learning about your style:

1. Pair up with someone that you trust. Ask them to observe you for five minutes on two occasions in the course of a working session, and to give you feedback on what you did. As you do not know when your partner is observing you, you will not be able to put on an act.

2. Use a fixed video to record a supervision session (the person who you are supervising must agree to this). To review your work style with a colleague whom you trust, look at how you acted and the effect that this had upon the person whom you are supervising.

Chapter Eighteen

Supervision and Management

This chapter explores:
- **Line management:** the whole management structure and process.
- **Managerial supervision meetings:** meetings between the manager and the worker which focus on the worker's past, present and future work.
- Issues of **discipline** and **competence**.

The Line Management Process

Case Study: Mary and Tim

Mary was a part-time worker in charge of a project on an estate where many young people had low self esteem. She had a part-time team to work with young people (15–23 years) to offer activities that would raise their confidence and personal skills. The project offered specific programmes in numeracy, literacy and IT. The job was very stressful. Her employers recognised this and offered support by 'popping round' very regularly. They valued her work and told her so.

One day, out of the blue, her manager **Tim** went into work and found a hand-written note pushed through his letter box.

Dear Tim,

I want to resign. I don't feel I'm doing the best I can for young people or the estate and also I'm very tired. Maggie would do the job well.

Mary.

Tim was gobsmacked. He knew Mary was stressed but had not seen this coming. He tried to phone her but the phone was off the hook. He phoned her colleague Maggie, and discovered that nothing special had happened the night before but Mary had been a bit upset. Someone suggested he sent her some flowers and a note asking if she wanted to talk. The response was almost instant. In a long phone call, Mary told Tim that she felt stressed all the time but found it impossible to handle difficult situations when:

a) She had to write reports. She was good at accounts but felt inadequate at writing, highlighted by the fact that she had not passed any exams at school. She disliked computers, so avoided the word processor. She knew what she wanted to say but found it impossible to commit it to paper.

b) Macca, Pete and Steve were around again. They were three young people with whom she had no positive relationship. She disliked them, and they knew it. They spent all their time winding her up, and she felt guilty, and as if she'd failed them, because she could not relate to them.

c) In supervision with her part-time team, Mary felt that:
- Some of the team were better at the job than her, and she had nothing to offer.
- She didn't feel comfortable supervising people, and it either became a chat, an inquisition or she spent most of the supervision time talking.
- It was awkward, as they were all friends too.

After a particularly difficult time with the three young men, and with a report deadline coming up, Mary decided to resign.

Tim's approach was straightforward and positive. He asked if he could delay dealing with her resignation, as she was such a valuable worker. He advised her to take some time off on sick leave. After this, they could talk again, and Mary could contact him in the meantime, if there was anything else she wished to discuss.

Mary did not resign. Tim used some of his limited budget to provide her with non-management supervision. Between them, they found a way forward: Lucinda, the project's IT tutor, would be paid to work with Mary on her reports to develop her IT skills. Mary developed confidence to use word processing functions and discovered the delights of spelling and grammar checks as well as the copy and paste functions!

After much soul searching, Tim realised that if Mary did not know how to supervise this could be because his supervision of her was not effective. He consulted with all the people he supervised, about his supervision style, and their own training needs as supervisors in their own right. He then used the last of the training budget to put on a day's workshop on supervision. This was followed up by regular reviews of the supervision process being built into the area team meetings. Tim became a better supervisor and role model for his staff, and the quality of the area's supervision rose. Staff felt better supported, and Tim did not need to 'pop in' as often to see his staff: they could get on with their work more effectively.

Mary's staff worked to keep Macca, Pete and Steve away from Mary in all but positive situations, thus helping to contain the problem until the three young men moved on of their own accord.

Mary gained insight into how to become a more effective manager. The job was still stressful but the stress was now manageable.

There are some learning points from Mary's story:
- The role of her manager was the key in helping her to identify and deal with her stress, even if it was late in coming.
- Mary needed an outsider to help her distance herself from the issues, and to work at solutions.
- The team Mary managed had a support role to play.
- Mary had not adjusted her thinking to that of being a manager. This is in itself stressful. She needed space and support to think about her work role.

The crisis of Mary's resignation pushed Tim into action. He became a good line manager. Line management is a continuous process by which the manager:

- directs
- supports
- motivates
- protects

- checks the work of
- provides opportunities for systematic review
- consults and passes information to and from the worker.

Every time the manager and the worker make contact by telephone, fax, e-mail, letter, memo or in person, line management is taking place. Even when there is no contact, the line management is in play. If you do not believe this, listen to workers' comments on their managers:

She knew it was going to be a difficult session, we'd talked about it the day before, but she never phoned to see how it went.

He tells me how important I am to the team. If I was that important, I reckon he'd occasionally take notice of the things I say. What's the point of being all nice when we have a supervision session and then doing naff-all about anything I say.

He's a good boss, he drops by when he's passing, he always comes along when he's needed, but he doesn't crowd me.

She's a funny woman. When I haven't seen her for a bit, I come in and find an e-mail with a cartoon on it, that's spot on for what's happening and I know she's up to speed.

One part of this process is called management supervision. This is a session where the manager and worker meet in private and work through an agreed agenda that focuses on the workers past, present and future work. Management supervision usually lasts between three-quarters to one hour and takes place every six to eight weeks. Management supervision is an important part in the line management process because this is the time when systematic, unhurried, review of the worker's work takes place. After a management supervision session, the worker should feel:

- valued
- thoughtful
- supported

- clearer about the work
- motivated
- that they have learned from the session

The pattern of contact may look something like Figure 17:

The line management process consists of meeting two sets of needs:

- the needs of the organisation
- the needs of the work

and dealing with the personal chemistry between the manager and the worker, see Figure 18.

Good line management is like a three ringed circle. All three areas need to be in balance. Equal attention must be paid to each area. If the manager focuses on just one area then there will be problems.

If the focus is on the needs of the organisation, then the manager will be seen to be authoritarian and uncaring. This is de-motivating for the worker who will feel devalued.

If the focus is on the needs of the worker then the manager has become the worker's mentor, counsellor or trainer. This will result in the manager finding it difficult

Figure 17: Pattern of possible contact between a worker in charge and a one-session-a-week worker

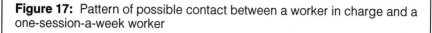

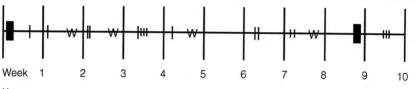

Week   1   2   3   4   5   6   7   8   9   10

Key:

■ : Managed supervision   W : Co-working session   ‖ : Contact sessions
(length of line shows importance)
e.g. e-mail, phone calls or face-to-face

Figure 18: Balancing needs in good line management

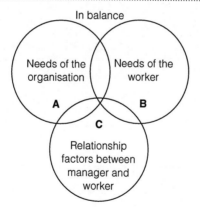

In balance

Needs of the organisation

Needs of the worker

A   B

C

Relationship factors between manager and worker

Imbalancing that can happen in the management/worker relationship

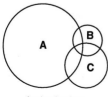

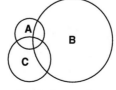

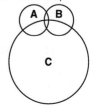

Authoritarian   Mentor/counsellor   Lovers or at war

to move back into the area of the needs of the organisation when this is required. Inevitably, there will be times when the manager has to say 'no' or 'I'm afraid that isn't acceptable or of the right quality' in which case the worker will feel betrayed.

If the focus is on the relationship between the manager and the worker then either they are close friends or at war. Neither of these positions is a good basis for line management as the needs of the organisation may be ignored. The result is that the young people lose out.

The way to discover how those you supervise see you has been discussed in detail earlier. A very simple way is to offer the person you supervise the model in Figure 19.

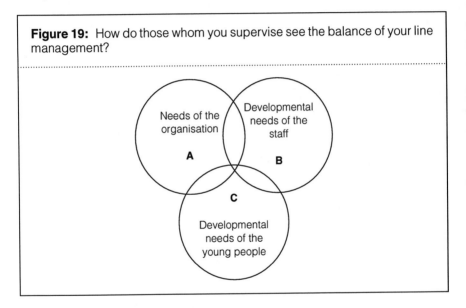

Figure 19: How do those whom you supervise see the balance of your line management?

Then ask the question 'If the size of the circles represents the time we spend together:
1. Which circle is the biggest, A, B or C?
2. Which is the smallest?
3. Is the balance right: how do you feel about this?'

Management Supervision Meetings

Many workers with management responsibilities tell us that the hardest parts of managing are the management supervision sessions, and they confide that they don't actually know what they should be doing. The result is the time is spent dealing with all the small decisions and administrative jobs that have built up over the last two or three months. This may be a useful 'clearing the decks session' but it is not management supervision. Further, it wastes a valuable opportunity for learning. In this spirit, here are some guidelines for a session.

As with all skilled work the quality of the work is dependent upon good solid preparation, so arrangements are important:

1. Fix a time and place where you can meet which is acceptable to both of you.

2. Make sure it is:
- private
- comfortable, i.e. warm and airy with soft seats of the same height
- uninterrupted, i.e. switch off mobile phones and put a 'do not disturb' sign on the door.

Agree start and finish times well before the session.

3. Ensure that you have produced and circulated the notes of the last meeting, together with the list of items that occur at every management supervision session. This is called the **standing agenda** (some organisations have particular proformas that must be used).

The standing agenda might be:

1) Achievements: things to be proud of which have occurred since the last meeting (too often difficulties and problems are focused on, and achievements forgotten).

2) The work which was to be carried out after the last meeting:
- What happened?
- What helped the work?
- What blocked the work?
- What was learned from this?
- Have any learning needs been identified?
- What does either manager or worker need to do as a result of this?

3) What is the social and economic situation of the young people being worked with: has anything changed in their locality?

4) If the person being supervised manages others, how are each of the people they manage developing?

5) In the light of the responses to the first four items of the standing agenda, what are the plans, objectives and tasks for the next period of time (say four months)?

6) What major things are happening in the next period, for example inspections, audit, annual report, advertisements for staff, staff holidays?

7) What help and support are needed to achieve nos. 5) and 6). Where is the support coming from: is the support framework working?

8) What do the manager and worker need to talk about in their relationship?

4. Read through the notes of the last meeting and put other things out of your mind. Your focus should be the person you are about to supervise, their work and their development.

5. Arrive early and check that the room is right, drinks are available and that you are focused.

6. Ensure that the supervisee, the person whom you are supervising, feels comfortable. If they are late do not just dive in to make up for lost time, allow them time to relax. If they arrive early, resist the temptation to use the time to deal with administrative business. If you say things like 'just glance at this before we start…sign these pay claims, please' it wrecks your focus, both yours and your supervisee's.

7. Start the session by asking the worker if there is anything they feel they need to talk about, before you start on the agenda. This is called 'getting rid of baggage'. Examples of baggage might be good or bad news that has just arrived; a bad journey before the session; the events last night. It is important that you do not let this baggage hijack the meeting.

8. Ask what items the worker would like on the agenda.

9. Add your own items.

10. Order the agenda so the standing items can be covered and then as many of the other items as possible; they may weave together comfortably. If it is obvious that one item is very large and may take the full session to deal with, arrange a separate meeting for this item at the earliest possible date.

11. Work through the agenda. Talk as little as possible and listen as much as possible. Do not give solutions: help the worker to find their solutions. After all, they are going to have to put the work into practice. Give positive feedback wherever possible. The process of coming to a solution may involve constructive criticism (see Chapter 17).

12. Make a note of what was discussed, who agreed to do what and the date it will be done by.

13. At the end, check out how the worker feels about the session.

14. Confirm the date of your next line management session, and the process by which you will agree the notes of the meeting you have just had.

15. Relax together for a few minutes, have a tea or coffee, and then go your separate ways.

If you supervise in this systematic manner you won't go far wrong, especially if you review your supervision sessions with your own supervisor and learn from the process. Good luck!

Managing Workers Who are in Difficulties

Managing workers who are skilled, confident and enthusiastic is relatively easy. Being a manager can never only be about motivating people, giving positive feedback and helping them to grow. Inevitably there will be occasions when you have to say things like:

No. I know it's a good idea, but we haven't got the resources to do it.

No, you can't go ahead with the trip: we've got to get parental consent forms and we can't even drive round to get them. I've tried phoning and no-one is in.

I need to talk to you. The young people are saying that you had a beer with them in the pub when you stopped for people to go to the toilet and then you drove the bus: what actually happened?

We need to talk. You seem very unhappy in your work. It's beginning to affect your relationships with young people…

These situations are always difficult. If you have a well-established relationship and a pattern of supervision this should help you. Be assertive and honest. Listen to the worker's concerns. However, you are appointed, and paid, to manage the situation. It is you that must make the decision and deal with the outcomes. There is nothing worse than being managed by someone who will not make decisions. Do so as reasonably and fairly as you can, balancing all the factors.

It is a different matter managing workers who are not doing the job that they are being paid to do. This group falls into broad categories, though some people may fall into more than one category. Those who refuse to follow procedures, lack skills, are insensitive, or only in youth work for their own ends.

Refusing to follow procedures

They do such things as regularly arrive late, never complete the paperwork for visits off-base or allow young people into the employer's premises whom they know have illegal drugs with them. This creates problems for their colleagues, who then become de-motivated if these matters are not dealt with.

Lacking skills

Workers may be aware of needing skills in an area of their work. They avoid those areas in which they feel that they are failing. Examples of such areas include dealing with conflict or working with certain age groups and failing to challenge oppression in all its forms. The effect is that others have to take on the work with the consequence that they can become resentful and or de-motivated. The quality of the work offered suffers.

Are insensitive

Such workers may not acknowledge the signals of young people and colleagues, and may continue to do things the way they have always done them. This happens even if it is against policy, or not relevant, or appropriate to the young people. These people offer poor role models, and can cause friction in the team, so that the quality of the work suffers.

Are only in youth work for their own ends

This might be thieves casing the joint, people recruiting young people to a particular political or religious belief, or paedophiles looking for prey. These individuals put young people at great risk.

As a manager, it is your responsibility to identify the workers who are in difficulty, and to work out exactly what the problem is. You then have to either help them become adequate workers who can do the job they are employed to do or ensure that they leave the job. In some cases, it is possible to counsel people so they leave with their self esteem intact and move positively to something else. In the most difficult cases, workers leave after disciplinary or competency hearings, warnings and finally dismissal or court cases.

It is always tempting to do nothing and hope the problems will go away. They will not. These matters are difficult to deal with, and stressful, and managers do not always get the support to do it that they need in turn from their senior managers. However, if you do not deal with these situations, it will still be stressful, and probably for longer. It is not in the best interests of the young people, your colleagues, the unit or ultimately your organisation, for you to leave the matter. It will kipper you.

How to deal with these problems

1. If you believe that what is happening is deliberate, and possibly criminal, or puts young people at risk, you must:
   - Contact your line manager at the earliest possible moment.
   - Record what has happened. Remember to put the time and date of the incident(s) and names of witnesses on the report. Sign it and record the time and date when you wrote it.
   - If you suspect it to be criminal, you must contact the police.
2. As with other problems, once you are aware that there is a difficulty, you must talk to the person concerned quietly, immediately and privately.
   - Do not jump to conclusions or make judgements before they are carefully and thoroughly investigated.
   - Say what you think the problem is.
   - Ask the worker to respond.

If you both agree that there is a problem, explain the effect of what is happening and ask how the worker thinks that the matter might be resolved.

For instance:

You: *John, I've noticed that for the last two weeks, you've arrived after seven. Everyone is expected to be there for 6.45. Is there a problem?*

John: *Yeah, sorry: it won't happen again.*

You: *Fine, it would be good if you could do this because it's beginning to make other people feel that it's unfair and that you are treated differently.*

Or John: *I've been waiting for you to say something. It's because in July and August there are no night shifts while they clean the factory. So I have to work to 6.30.*

In this case you have an explanation and can decide what to do.

You: *Dave, we've discussed this several times before. It's not OK to shout things like 'Get your arse into gear you little f...' and things like that when you are having a kick about in the park. I know the kids do it but we have to show them that there are other ways. You're a role model.*

Dave: *OK boss.*

In which case you can be positive in supervision, and try to move him on some more.

Or Dave: *F... off what do you know.*

If you get the latter response you must consider disciplinary proceedings.

You: *Kerry I've noticed that you spend a lot of time in the office on the phone, is there a problem?*

Kerry: *Sorry, my mum's ill and it's the only time I can phone her: do you want me to pay for the calls?*

Or it might transpire that Kerry is quite afraid of dealing with aggression, so she hides in the office. In this case you can begin to develop a strategy that will help her be more confident and effective.

Each of these interventions has moved the problem on. Following this initial contact:

- Record what happened: time, place, date and time of writing should be included. Keep this document secure.
- Read through the disciplinary procedures so that you are familiar with it in case you need it.
- Do not keep checking up on the worker in a way that they feel that they are being harassed.
- Be supportive to the worker and offer positive feedback where you can.
- With luck and hard work the problem will be resolved.

3. If the problem reoccurs, or what you agreed is not happening after a reasonable time then you must raise the matter again. These events fall into two categories:

Matters of discipline:

Dave, for instance, in the example above, was not following instructions or procedures, so this is a disciplinary matter.

- Ask to see Dave privately, and inform him that his work is not satisfactory.
- Explain the reason why it is unsatisfactory, and the effect this has on the unit, staff and young people. Ask him to respond.
- If there is no reasonable explanation, tell him clearly what is expected of him and that the matter will become a formal disciplinary matter if his conduct continues.
- Offer him help and support in resolving the matter while continuing to work.
- Tell him that you are recording the meeting and give him a copy of your records together with a copy of the disciplinary procedure for his information.
- After the meeting, be supportive, give positive feedback where you can, do not hassle him, which can be construed as harassment.
- Inform your manager of the situation. It is to be hoped that the problem will not reoccur. If it does you will need to consider formal disciplinary proceedings against Dave, and you will need to discuss this with your manager before you take any action.

Matters of competence

An example of this is Kerry, still hiding from any aggression or confrontation. Here you will need to see the training officer or your manager ,and discuss ways that you might support Kerry to develop the skills she needs.

- Ask to see Kerry privately. Explain that the problem does not seem to have resolved itself, and you would like to work out with her a package that will help her to develop the required skills. The package might include:
  - Working with an experienced worker who would not just protect her, but will help her to begin to deal with the issues.
  - Attending an in-service training course on *Assertiveness* or *Handling Conflict.*
  - Ensuring that she has at least one area where she works with a less demanding group so she can achieve success.
- Agree to a date when the outcomes of the package will be reviewed. Record the meeting and give Kerry a copy.
- Afterwards, be supportive, give positive feedback where you can, and do not hassle her.
- Hold the review meeting, perhaps inviting any other workers involved and assess progress. It is to be hoped that there will be some. Decide what the next step will be.
- If there is no progress, then set up a second programme with a review date. Record the meeting and give the worker a copy.
- Talk to your line manager. If there is still no progress after the second developmental programme, you and your line manager need to consider competency proceedings.

In both cases, at the end of these procedures, the matter is then in the hands of senior managers, who may or may not act quickly. They may not want to act at all. If so:

- Keep recording.
- Keep asking your manager for help and advice in the matter in writing.
- Raise the issues at your supervision meetings with your manager.
- Keep informing the worker that their work is not satisfactory, why it is not satisfactory and what you expect of them.
- Be supportive to the worker and do not hassle or bully them.

Look after yourself during all of these processes:

- Keep up your other work. Ensure the quality is as high as possible.
- Never be rude, sarcastic or offensive, treat the worker with respect.
- Never gossip about what is happening.
- Use your supportive framework (see Chapter 16)
- *Hang in there.*

This may all seem very formal and not at all how a youth worker should work, but it should achieve the following:

- Protect young people and ensure the high quality service they need and deserve.
- Dealing with the situation.
- Sending messages to your colleagues, and manager, that you expect the work to be of reasonable quality.
- Establishing your role as a staff developer (see Chapter 19).
- Stopping you being **kippered**.

Chapter Nineteen

Staff Development

Identifying Worker's Learning Needs

In order to help youth workers to develop their skills, knowledge, beliefs and attitudes, it is necessary to identify the areas that need development. Our list of key competencies set out below, may help you in the process. However, your organisation probably has documents that sets out what an individual should know and be able to do in order to qualify as a part-time youth worker and a list of competencies that full-time youth workers should demonstrate in their probationary year. This list may be quite different from the one offered here, or that offered by PAULO. This is because of the emphasis that this book places on identifying need, and the development of systematic, planned work and its evaluation.

Key areas of competency of youth workers.

There are many more **competencies**; this list contains some of the most essential abilities:

- Build and maintain a safe learning climate.
- Work in a participatory way.
- Understand prejudice and its effects, and work to counter it.
- Form and maintain relationships with a wide range of young people in order to move them towards autonomy.
- Afterwards, exit from the relationship to help young people move on.
- Work in at least two different youth work settings.
- Understand what young people need to know, are able to do and are predisposed towards in order to become effective adults, for example, communication abilities, decision making skills, relationship building skills, staying healthy, independent living, finding and holding work, education or training, looking after the environment and its people, countering prejudice, living safely, etc.
- Identify young people's learning needs.
- Design and deliver planned programmes to meet these needs.
- Understand how groups function (their roles, norms, controls, group dynamics and processes) and use this understanding to work both with groups and to offer learning about groups.
- Work one-to-one with a young person, befriending them, giving information, and advice where this is required.

- Signpost young people on to other services to have their needs met, when and wherever it is more appropriate.
- Monitor, review and evaluate work.
- Help young people to learn from their experiences.
- Use oneself as a way of offering learning (coaching, modelling and instructing).
- Think systematically and creatively and be able to use these skills in the work.
- Understand the issues of equality of opportunity, health and safety, and child protection, and use the principles of these to underpin the work.
- Be a contributing team member.
- Understand and implement the policy of the organisation.
- Hold current appropriate skill certificates including first aid and those required to undertake specialist activities, e.g. from the sports governing body or from drama, dance or craft organisations.
- Write reports and references for young people.
- Handle money in accordance with the organisation's financial regulations.
- Manage oneself in order to keep time, and boundaries, and to focus on work when at work.
- Prepare for management supervision and respond to it where necessary.
- Be supportive to colleagues and develop own support framework.
- Identify own learning and developmental needs and work to meet these.

One method of helping workers to identify their **learning needs** is to focus on an area of competence in management supervision, and explore what it means in a range of situations. Next, identify the range of skills and knowledge that a worker has in this area. Finally, select one skill that the worker could develop, and work out an action plan to ensure that this development occurs.

Alternatively co-work with a skilled individual. This gives both workers opportunities to observe each other at first hand and thus identify learning needs. The workers also identify their learning needs through ongoing reflection, review and evaluation of their work.

Meeting the Needs

This process should be very similar to the youth work process, and it is important that it is, for two reasons:

1. The youth worker can learn how to offer learning to young people by reflecting on the way learning is offered to them, and how they are encouraged to grow and develop.
2. It ensures that there is coherence throughout the whole of the organisation and also between theory and practice.

To keep the staff development process in balance with the needs of the young people and the organisation:

- The worker and manager work together to identify the worker's learning needs and how these can be met.

- They decide which needs are best met by off-the-job training and which can be met through on-the-job training.
- The manager then balances the learning needs of all staff together with the needs of the organisation and the general needs of young people.
- The manager develops the programme in a way that gives workers on-the-job training in their areas of need through:
  - New experiences.
  - Co-working opportunities.
  - Coaching, modelling and instructing.

  This process is supported by management supervision. If possible, the needs of the staff, the young people, and the organisation can be met in one activity.
- Sometimes it is only possible to combine two areas: for A and B (staff development and needs of the organisation), this might occur when workers write and present reports, complete fund-raising applications, help plan a programme, handle money and participate in team meetings and awaydays.

  To combine areas A and C (staff development and young people's needs) consider any activities that take place as part of the unit programme but which do not have a direct impact on it or the outside world, for example, information giving, problem solving, befriending, arts and crafts, drama, trips and visits, health education and other projects.
- The manager and the worker then identify the worker's learning development in line management sessions and set new targets.
- Some learning needs are met in off-the-job supervision. In this case the line management focuses on:
  - What the worker learned.
  - How this can be applied in the worker's work.
  - How the rest of the team can benefit from the worker's experience.
- Worker's achievements should be recorded in some sort of a log book so that they can be used by the worker in job applications and be a permanent record of success, that might otherwise be forgotten. This is an extension of the portfolio system of youth work training.

Case Study: The unit's contribution to the local gala

Defining the Needs
The unit's needs: to raise its profile in the local community
   The activity has the potential to meet these needs.

Staff development needs:
Stu: to take responsibility for a complete piece of work.
Alex: to work with adults, not just young people.
Ron: to help less experienced workers on-the-job.
Simone: to see systematic needs-led work in action.
   Stu works with a small group to enter the raft race. It is the first project where he has taken sole responsibility. Alex attends the gala planning meeting with four young people. Not only is it the first time that he has represented

the unit to the outside world but it is the first time that he has helped young people speak on their own behalf in a completely adult situation.

Ron and Simone run the fancy dress competition for the under-7s with a team of young people. It is the first time Ron has been the most experienced worker when co-working. Simone is a new worker and this is her first experience of systematic planning based on identification of needs.

Young people's needs:
The group involved in the raft race are not high achievers. They have low self esteem and little confidence. They find it hard to co-operate with each other, and neither do they relate well to older adults whom they see as 'stiffs'. Their needs are to:

- Have new experiences.
- Successfully complete a project to a timescale.
- Perform in public.
- Learn to work as a team.
- Cope with frustrations and failure.
- Overcome problems.
- Be recognised as successful.
- Gain in confidence.

The group on the gala planning committee are a group of young women who do not recognise their own talents and worth. They see themselves as children. They need to:

- Be treated as adults and work in an adult world.
- Be involved in formal committees.
- Speak in public.
- See the complexity of organising a big event (even if they find it a bit boring at times, they say that they want their picture in the paper)!

The fancy dress competition group had been seen as difficult and irresponsible by their community. They experienced:

- Being seen in a different role.
- Having fun without excess.
- Being publicly thanked.
- Achieving success.
- Taking responsibility for others.

Assessing the Outcomes: How the Needs Were Met
The needs of the organisation:
The project worked well to raise the unit's profile. The wider community were impressed by the enthusiasm that the youth workers brought to the event.

An unforeseen bonus was that the Youth work process no longer took place behind closed doors. The workers talked about their objectives for the young people's learning, their frustrations, failures and successes. Some members of the community saw the process in action, recognised the difficulty of the work, and saw the development of the young people.

The staffs' learning needs:
Stu gained confidence as the project progressed. At first he needed to discuss each development with the worker in charge. By the day of the race, Stu had accepted that he was responsible for the piece of work and had learned to distinguish what actually needed to be referred to the worker in charge and what he should deal with himself.

Alex's comment at the end of the gala was, 'I learned more than the kids about working with adult committees, and what's more I've discovered that

I'm an adult! But the young women were tremendous, weren't they...they are flying.'

Ron found the whole process extremely difficult. 'I do what I do because I know what to do. I've never tried to explain it before. Simone is great, relates to the kids well but I had to explain everything...It was hard to get her to focus on the process, she was so taken up in the relating. I didn't do my bit very well...I could do it better now though. I should have been more sorted out at the beginning. Simone likes things written down... I tend to skip that bit. Next time I'll take my trainer role more seriously at the start.'

Simone said, 'It was only at the end that I realised where we'd been and how we'd gone on a pathway from the idea to the competition...and on the way the young people had grown. Up 'til then I thought learning just happened by chance and we related to the young people because it helped them to get involved. It's exciting to realise that its all planned...its good when a plan comes together.'

The young people's needs:
These were extensively met, there was too much learning to record it in detail here.

...And the results...
The raft sank but the group crossed the finish line, swimming with their floats held high accompanied by cheers from the crowd. The group on the planning committee did get their pictures in the paper.

They have now left the unit and have became involved in the peace movement.

The fancy dress competition was successful, 40 children entered. The group had only brought prizes for the 25 who had entered before the day. The owner of the local sweet shop from where the group stole regularly, donated the 15 remaining prizes. He still laughs when he recalls the desperate young man saying, 'Help us please...it's not for us, it's for the little kids...and they don't nick from you, do they?' The group never stole from that shop again and were proud of their achievements. Three still come to the unit.

And the worker in charge said to her manager, 'no-one thinks I did anything. They don't remember the hours I spent on the phone or talking over problems. They never know about the 'backstopping' and behind-the-scenes repair work that I did...still, that's staff development for you...'

What is Staff Development?

Staff development is the process during their employment, by which the worker grows in knowledge, skills and attitudes, and gains in experience.

> *I came into this job straight from college. I'd been a part-time worker for four years and I was good at it but the first six months were the steepest learning curve in my life. If it hadn't been for good supervision, a supportive team and the induction programme, I know that I'd have developed really bad habits...blamed others...hidden when I should have been out there...pretending that I was coping...bullshitting...you know.*

...What I learned was...how to learn from my work. I hope it stays with me. Every day I learn some new thing. I try to go on a course every year and some conferences. Meetings to keep me up to date...most of all I learn from reviewing my work.

(JNC 3 worker)

Staff development is a learning process. If you are a manager you are responsible for the staff development of all those you manage. It is important that you understand how people learn (Chapter 6) and put this knowledge into practice. The principles are the same for young people and adults. Staff development starts at interview. It continues until the worker leaves the organisation. It has many parts and to explore it in detail would take a book in itself. This chapter can do no more than give you an insight into the process. You can then expand your knowledge and skill through your own staff development by:

- Reading the staff development policy of your organisation and discussing with your manager how you put it into operation.
- Reading books and articles.
- Reviewing your work as a staff developer both in management supervision sessions and with colleagues.
- Asking those you manage for their comments.
- Asking for your own staff development needs to be met through on and off-the-job training. Ensure that the training has ample skill development.
- Thinking about the staff development that you have received, note what worked for you, what did not and what would have been useful if it had been in place. This will give you insight into good staff development practices and also how you learn.

Understanding staff development and its component parts

The whole process of staff development has to be carried out within a framework of equal opportunities and in a safe learning climate, see Figure 20. It is very difficult to learn if you are oppressed, or feel unsafe.

The process of staff development begins at interview and ends only when the individual exits from the post. When a person begins a new job they must be inducted into the organisation. They need to know:

- What is expected of them.
- How the organisation works.
- The people, and who does what.
- The policies, practices and procedures that define the job.

They also need opportunities to demonstrate the knowledge, skills and abilities that they bring with them. This can then be fitted into the organisation's pattern of work, in a way that benefits young people.

After induction there are a number of strands that are bound together as a rope, management supervision and support, team development, personal development, job development, appraisal and on and off-the-job training.

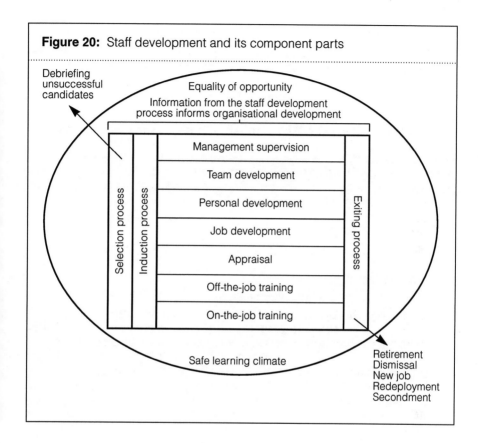

Figure 20: Staff development and its component parts

Management supervision and support

These have already been discussed in detail (Chapter 18).

Team development

This refers to the worker's contribution to the team. The whole team plays a role in supporting and developing its members. A good team should have a major impact on staff development. This is why a safe learning climate and the ability to challenge and debate is so important. It is here that workers gain knowledge and insight into the youth work process.

Personal development

Growth in confidence and self esteem, the ability to think and develop sensitivity, empathy and a flexible personal style, are all parts of personal development.

Job development

This is concerned with the post holder being able to take on more and develop new areas once he or she has got to know the job, settled in and built a firm base.

Appraisal

Not all organisations undertake appraisals. It is the time at which the manager formally lets the worker knows how the organisation views them. The reason for this process is that all managers have views about the performance of the people whom they manage. It follows that it is only fair if these are formally recorded and not held as judgemental hearsay. This gives the worker the opportunity to comment on the record, should that be necessary.

Off-the-job training

This refers to courses, conferences and workshops that the worker attends.

On-the-job training

The methods used for on-the-job training are:

- **Modelling:** The learner observes another worker (the model) at work. The model must be able and prepared to discuss what happened, why they acted as they did and what was or was not effective. It helps if the model is skilled at linking practice to theory and can set their actions in the context of their value base.
- **Instructing:** Explaining and demonstrating tasks. This requires great judgement in deciding how much freedom to give the learner to develop their own style and how much they should be asked to develop in the instructor's image. It also requires great clarity on the part of the instructor.
- **Coaching:** Coaching in work is the same as in sport. It is the practice of skills, in a safe situation. It involves extending the range of skills and of breaking down sequences of events to find and strengthen the weakest points. Coaching is usually achieved through role play, socio-drama and other practical activities.
- **Co-working:** Working with an experienced individual who helps the learner to develop as an equal partner, is achieved through a mixture of modelling, instructing, coaching, reviewing the work they do together and reviewing each of their contributions.
- **Exiting:** This is the process by which someone:
  - Closes their current work.
  - Closes their work relationships.
  - Identifies their achievements and developments in the post.
  - Feeds back to the organisation what they see as the organisation's strengths and weaknesses.
  - Gets ready to move on.

At the end of this process, there is usually a meal or party, the achievements of the leaver are formally recognised and goodbyes are said.

Case Study: Kev's staff development pathway

> **Kev** was a young man whom the detached work team came across occasionally between the time he was 15 to just before his 17th birthday. He was friendly, unreliable and a pot user. The team helped him through various problems, including trouble with the police and homelessness. They also helped get him to a dentist when he had an abscess. He then disappeared.
>
> Five years later, aged 22, he turned up saying, 'I want to be a youth worker. I want to do for others what you did for me.' His staff development process started.
>
> **The Selection Process**
> **Ken**, the detached team leader explained that there were no part-time vacancies so he could not apply for any jobs at the moment. He could be a volunteer if he wanted but that he would have to apply, be interviewed and cleared by the police before he started work. Ken also explained the difference between part- and full-time qualifications and they had a conversation about his future intentions.
>
> A month later, Kev had been interviewed by Ken, as well as the Area Youth Manager and a member of the management committee. He was accepted. His police clearance took some time, as he had received a caution for being in the possession of cannabis. This was some six years ago, however, and as there was nothing else on his record the organisation decided to accept him. He was given a job description and he started work as a volunteer.
>
> **Induction**
> Ken arranged for Kev to go on a series of visits over the first six months. These included:
> - The youth forum.
> - The area meetings of the part-time youth workers.
> - Team meetings.
> - Observing a council meeting following a visit to the Education Department.
>
> Ken also explained to Kev about policies and showed him those on opportunities, staff development, the outreach/detached work, and drugs.
>
> Kev worked with Franklyn, a very experienced detached worker. He explained the purpose of their work and how to go about it. He also showed Kev how to handle money, including petty cash, complete nightly report forms and accident report forms. They co-worked for some eight months.
>
> During this time, Kev decided he wanted to go to college and study to be a full-time worker. He thought he would stay with the team for two years after finishing his induction. During this time he would do some GCSEs.
>
> **Management Supervision**
> Ken was his management supervisor. He helped Kev to see the importance of:
> - Identifying young people's needs.

- Working systematically to meet the needs.
- Evaluating the outcomes.
- Reviewing work.

The hardest part was getting Kev to think things through. He had never thought systematically before, just reacted or acted. The process was slow but the co-working with Franklyn provided experiences that acted as a basis for his learning.

On-the-job Training

Franklyn helped Kev improve his listening skills and skills in talking to a range of people: young people, teachers, counsellors and the police. Franklyn also helped with his writing and numeracy skills: he used report writing and returns as the basis for this work. Kev became quite motivated when he saw it was all necessary for him to get to College.

Off-the-job Training

In his first year Kev attended courses on:

- Child protection: 2 evenings
- ABC first aid: 2 evenings
- Drugs awareness: 1 evening
- A team awayday: 1 day
- Introduction to Part-time Youth Work: 6 evenings

He enjoyed the training, contributed well and was proud of his certificates.

Support

Ken used a supervision session to explain about a support framework and encouraged Kev to set one up and use it, which he did, more or less. Kev was always inclined to turn to his mates in times of trouble.

Personal Development

Kev grew in confidence and at the end of the year took a short *Return to Learning* course. His personal style became more flexible generally. He was now prepared to modify his appearance to achieve desired outcomes, if the situation required it. He became less aggressive, and more assertive.

Year One: Career Development

At the end of that first year, he wrote off to colleges that did youth work courses for prospectuses. He arranged to visit a college and talked to the students. That motivated him enormously and made him see the importance of being successful in his *Return to Learning* course.

Job Development

By the end of the year, Kev had moved from just doing what Franklyn said, to planning small projects with his help. Finally, he reached the stage of running projects past Franklyn before he went ahead with his support.

Team Development
Kev's role in the team changed dramatically. He developed from a silent member to the dominator of air time. After a difficult line management session and supportive, but firm pressure from the team, he developed into an equal, more thoughtful contributor.

Appraisal
There was no formal system but both Franklyn and Ken gave Kev a great deal of feedback on how he was developing.

Line Management
This was mainly a smooth process. Ken talked to Kev very seriously about his timekeeping in the middle of the year, when he became very unreliable.

The major difficulty was over Kev's attitude to young people smoking pot. He felt that it was, 'Just a bit of blow: much less dangerous than booze'. Ken had to make it clear to Kev that as a youth worker he must never actively encourage the use of illegal substances or knowingly allow them on youth service premises. Kev was never happy about the drugs policy but accepted it grudgingly as the price for doing the job.

Organisational Development
Kev made a large contribution to changing the way the organisation trained its part-time workers. As a result of his experiences and recommendations *The bridge* was established, a short course for people who might be interested in youth work training but had little formal education. Kev also breathed life into the youth forum insisting that it was listened to.

Year Two: Career Development
A part-time vacancy arose in the detached team, Kev applied, was interviewed and got the job.

Kev applied to go to college with help from Franklyn and was accepted.

Induction
As Kev was now a paid worker he had to complete the full Local Authority induction that included far more on:
- Health and safety at work.
- Anti-oppressive practice.
- How the local authority worked.
- Disciplinary, grievance and competency procedures.

Job Development
Kev planned a residential weekend with a worker from another area. This was the first piece of work for which he had sole responsibility.

Off-the-job Training
As a result of Franklyn's coaching, modelling and associated discussions, Kev's style of work became extremely flexible as he became more aware of the effects he had on others.

Personal Development
Kev found a partner, and they rented a flat near the college he was going to attend. He completed his *Return to Learning* course successfully.

Management Supervision
This focused on:
- Setting targets.
- Reviewing movement towards the targets.
- Identifying learning and how this had come about.

Kev practised reading and writing in the job, using it as preparation for college.

Exiting
During Kev's last six weeks with the team, Ken took care to see that Kev had time to:
- Tie up the loose ends at work.
- Wind down relationships with the young people and staff.
- Formally identify his growth and achievements.
- Send a report to the council about his experiences. Kev recommended changes in the recruitment, training and support for workers. He felt it was important that trainees had the opportunity to work in a range of settings and not just in one job.

A leaving party was held to celebrate the end of the exiting process.

Ken also helped Kev cope with a crisis of confidence when Kev felt that he would not be able to cope at College.

Kev is now a successful full-time worker in a London Borough. He has two children and is enjoying life enormously. He still has not resolved his feelings about the drugs policies of his employers. In this respect he may be at risk.

Chapter Twenty

Managing your Manager

Managers are human, most of them are hard working and under pressure. Some are inspirational, creative and a source of learning. They all from time to time become tired, forget things, make mistakes and get bad tempered, as we all do. It follows that on occasions all workers are annoyed by the actions of their managers, sometimes because of something the manager has done, and sometimes by what they have not done. 'It's not replying to me that gets on my nerves, I write, phone, e-mail and fax, and what do I get? Nothing.' In order to minimise the potential frustration, it is necessary to manage your manager.

Remember that your manager has positional power (see Chapter 17). Never challenge your manager directly as if it comes to conflict you will always loose. You must find other strategies. The only exception to this is if you go into grievance procedures that is very different from the normal management process.

Strategies to Manage your Manager
Get to know your manager

Discover why your manager came into youth work. Originally almost everyone came into the job because they wanted to help young people and to make a difference. This wish does not go away, but opportunities to work with young people get less as you are promoted. If you can legitimately invite your manager to or involve them in an event with young people where they get a 'buzz' you may see a different side to them. You can talk together as youth workers. This will give a different dimension to your relationship as well as giving your manager a good experience and keeping him or her in touch with young people in today's world.

Try to see the world through your manager's eyes

Try acting in a way that minimises the stress on your relationship:

- Do that report, get the returns in on time. This will prevent your manager having to locate you to tell you they have not arrived. It will save them time and hassle.
- Let them know about the situation of young people with whom you work. Managers always feel safer when they have high quality up-to-date information to work from. It also means that they can advocate on behalf of young people more effectively.

- If there is a major problem, tell your manager as soon as possible and ask for advice. There is nothing worse from a manager's point of view than having their own manager, the press or a parent contacting them about something, when they know nothing of the matter. If this happens, your manager may be left feeling embarrassed and angry with you, regardless of the rights and wrongs of the matter.

Give your manager positive feedback and constructive criticism

They may not be getting any feedback at all, or worst still, most of it may be negative. Just a few words can make a difference to your relationship and how your manager feels about you:

> *Thanks for that.*
> *Thanks for responding so quickly.*
> *I've never thought of that, that's a great idea.*

If you are able to give more fulsome praise, so much the better:

> *Your support made a lot of difference.*
> *I know you've worked hard for us and you've got a result.*

Treat your manager as a valuable person

Give them 'put ups.' Ask them how they are. Listen to the answer. They may need to off-load their feelings. Make their working climate safe when they are with you.

When you need to talk to your manager, present yourself professionally

If you have a problem, define the problem clearly, and come up with some possible answers.

Case Study: Managing your manager

> Worker:
> *Parents on the estate want us to run a play scheme in the summer holidays. They asked me and I told them we have no money to pay staff and we are only supposed to work with over-13s. They've talked to their councillor and to the press. I think it might be in next week's Echo.*
> *As I see it there are three things we could do:*
> - *Do nothing: but there is a need and it's becoming high profile.*
> - *Find say 40 sessions for Hussain and Jackie to work with some senior members to do something for 10 days: there is a small group who are interested. We have had a vacancy for two months so there must be sessions in hand.*

- *Or I could spend a few sessions talking to the fire service, police, and the Health Team, etc., and see what I could put together with different agencies doing different things on different days as freebies. We've done something like this before and it's OK: it'd take me about a week to sort.*

Manager:

> *I'd prefer the second option if it's possible. I could give you statistics on the level of poverty on the estate together with two or three case studies if that would help you make a case to anyone.*

If you are making a case, present it with a well thought out and prepared argument.

Consider the questions that you may be asked and work out the answers to them. If you get a negative reply, accept it with good grace.

> *Oh well, thanks for spending time on it.*

Being bad tempered won't change the present decision, but it might just alter the state of mind of your manager to your next request.

Be prepared to compromise in disputes

If you have a dispute with your manager work for a **win–win** solution if this is possible, see Figure 21:

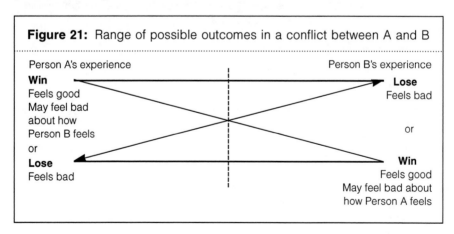

Figure 21: Range of possible outcomes in a conflict between A and B

The only way both A and B in Figure 21 can end up feeling good is in a win–win outcome. A win–win negotiation requires compromise, but it does leave everyone feeling positive. Prepare for the meeting thoroughly:

- Work out what your bottom line is, what can you not afford to give away.

- Try to work out why your manager holds the position they do. Are they being instructed by their manager, is it a matter of principle or belief, do they dislike you, or is the issue tied into other larger issues. Ask: this will help you to work out your manager's bottom line.
- Remember that you are the expert on your work and the young people with whom you work. Prepare evidence to support your position. It is helpful to practice ways of presenting this so your manager feels that you are making a helpful and informed contribution.

    I've got some figures that might help us...
    Here's two examples from last week. I've only just written them up...I've done you a copy.

- Consider if there is anything that your manager wants from you; might it be possible to do a trade off?

Once you have thought about these four areas you are in a position to develop a strategy for handling the meeting. Explore the strategy with someone on your support framework. If it is helpful, use role play to rehearse the strategy.

If the situation becomes tense and difficult then try to engineer a break. Sometimes it is possible to say, 'we seem to have reached a block, could we take a few moments?' This gives you time to think and you can come back with a more positive approach, and something that may work for both of you.

Never play games or try to wind your manager up

The style that works most effectively is thoughtful assertiveness and reasonableness. If you make a mistake, say so. There is nothing that makes anyone look more stupid than defending an indefensible position.

Act professionally at all times

Never respond by putting people down or devaluing them in any way. After the meeting, whatever the outcomes, never resort to bad-mouthing your manager or revealing confidential information. This cannot help the position. Find someone within your support framework that you can talk to about your feelings and who can help you reach a calm decision about what you are going to do next.

Grievance Procedures

If you feel that you are being treated unfairly or unprofessionally by your manager you can embark on a grievance procedure. Before you do:

- Read your organisation's Grievance Procedures carefully.
- Make sure that you have tried every other avenue first and that this is documented.
- Ensure that you have a well-documented case.
- Consider the possibility of a group action if you are not the only person to be affected by the matter.
- If you are not a union member consider joining before you take any action.

Grievance procedures are often countered by employers instigating disciplinary procedures against the employee. This usually expands the time of the conflict to well over a year. At the end of this time, you may be exhausted and no longer want to stay in the job. Don't let this stop you taking out a grievance, but just ensure that you have thought about the consequences of the action. Consider how stressful it will be and that the situation may go on for a long time. Make sure that you can survive this process. Get advice from a union before you do **anything**. It may be possible for a union representative to deal with the matter, without starting a grievance procedure.

No one has the right to:

- Treat you unprofessionally.
- Oppress you or discriminate against you.
- Belittle or insult you.
- Manage you in a way that prevents you from doing your job, or be consistently incompetent.
- Bully you.

If they do any of these things you should start grievance procedures about it. Thankfully these things do not happen often. It is usually possible to manage your manager using your skills, good humour and tolerance, and your professionalism.

Remember. It is important to let your manager manage you as well.

Chapter Twenty-one

Knowing your Organisation

Why Knowing your Organisation is Important

What is there to know? They send me bits of paper, I send them back filled in and they file them. Di comes round and visits sometimes. I like her, she's helpful. Oh yes, and every year around Christmas I get a letter from the Director telling me how invaluable I am. They always spell my name wrong... (Part-time worker)

Is this your relationship with your organisation? If it is, you may be missing out on things that could be useful to you, and which could provide additional resources for young people. Knowing your organisation should enable you to:

- **Keep up-to-date** with what is happening in your organisation, for example, what is their response to any new policies that affect young people.
- **Get help** and advice on a wide range of matters, including income generation, legal issues and publicity.
- **Involve** yourself in a way that can influence decisions made on behalf of young people.
- **Advise** young people how they can act on their own behalf or influence decisions.

Our project was strong on participation. We wanted to give the older young people real responsibility, including running their own bank account. The financial department said that we couldn't do that, because it wasn't in the regulations. We kept saying, that as the money was the young people's the Local Authority regulations shouldn't apply. I then found a bit in the Youth Service policy handbook. It said that the authority '...Actively encouraged young people to work towards taking control of all aspects of their lives in order to become effective adults...' We were then able to successfully argue that the young people's bank account was within our policy. (Part-time worker)

Knowing your organisation can also help you to:

1. Ensure that young people's needs are considered in other parts of the organisation. If you do not know about and engage with other sections of your organisation, you could be disadvantaging young people. You could miss out on:
    - Helping shape your organisation's policy and methods of working with young people. Face-to-face workers are the people who know about the reality of young people's lives and how they are changing. Policy makers need this information in order to make policy, and take decisions that are appropriate to young people's needs.

- Opportunities to be involved in new developments. This may bring with it additional resources and additional work.

2. Make yourself known and extend your influence. In the best of all worlds, each worker should have the chance to participate in all the opportunities that come along. However, the reality is often that time is short and so people are approached whom the management team know as individuals, think will be interested and will respond positively. Contact leads to involvement, positive involvement leads to more involvement and influence. This increases the range of opportunities available to the young people with whom you work.

3. Get advice, help, and resources. Most large organisations have a range of departments who may be able to offer you help or to signpost you to someone else:

> *We were doing a project on women's health and achievements. The library lent us about 30 books for a couple of weeks...I didn't know they could do this until I asked.* (Connexions worker)

> *I rang up the income generation people, just to see if we could get anything...on the off chance really. This bloke came out to see us and we finished up with a basket ball court, a hard play area and some equipment. It started as a basketball thing but now the young people run their own team and some of them are interested in being junior coaches.* (Full-time youth worker)

> *We knew that the council was going to change its policy about letting its buildings: schools, youth clubs, adult education centres, swimming pools etc... We were worried that they wouldn't put in special arrangements for youth groups. None of ours have much money. We rang up the Chief Exec.'s department and found out all about it. We then wrote to all the councillors and had a meeting with them. In the end they put in special rates for youth groups.* (Youth forum member)

If you need advice or information begin by asking colleagues and your line manager. Other departments may be busy and do not have time to answer questions to which the answers have already been given to someone, somewhere else in the youth department. If you cannot get an answer from inside the youth work department, then contact other departments directly. If you want help but don't know which department you need, ring the general line and ask the switch board operator to put you in touch with someone who deals with whatever it is you need to know about.

A word of advice: when you phone, have paper and pen to hand. Make a note of the name and extension number of the person you speak to. This will ensure that you can get back to the same person.

What is it Important to Know?

You will find it helpful to learn:

- The structure of your organisation.
- What each department in your organisation does.
- Individuals in each department. Real relationships, conducted over the phone or in person, not only make work more pleasant but can be of enormous help when there is a problem or you have a query.

- The process by which decisions are made, both in the whole organisation and in the youth service.
- Who the major policy and decision makers are and a little about their background and interests. This includes councillors, as well as members of management committees and steering groups.
- Consultation arrangements. Your young people and their community may want to contribute to these.
- The communication pathways. How information should get to you and from you to others: the official communication pathway.

There will also be unofficial communication pathways. You need to know this as well: the unofficial pathways are often more effective. They might be based on such things as:

- friendships
- people who share cars to work
- departments that share offices or work closely together
- groups that socialise after work
- family relationships

Case Study: Getting to the 'root' of youth work

A bit back it struck our team that none of the young people that we worked with knew anything about politics, local or national, or how to make their voices heard. We felt that political education was really important if they were to grow into independent adults, so we set up a three-strand strategy:

- *We established a strong youth council according to the authority's regulations.*
- *We ran lots of political education courses for young people. We made them fun and active but we showed them how to lobby and make their voices heard.*
- *We supported them when they wanted to take up an issue.*

This took three years. Young people and decision makers now expect young people will be involved.

They were involved in:

- *Making statements about unemployment.*
- *Lobbying on behalf of other young people.*
- *Objecting to the closure of the primary school in the village: it would have destroyed the village.*

At first it was very hard, the organisation wanted to stop us even though we were within the policy and regulation. They kept on checking us. The auditors audited us and an HMI was sent on a visit to us. We survived despite all of this attention. When they saw nothing awful happened they had to resign themselves to us being on the scene.

We couldn't have done it if we hadn't kept to those precautions [listed below]. At one point we nearly lost our jobs: but it was worthwhile

(Full-time youth worker)

If you decide to work 'at the root' there are a number of precautions that you should take to keep you safe:

- Make sure that young people feel the matter is important to them. You have no right to use young people to fight your own political beliefs. Collect evidence on the matter they wish to address and make sure that young people are part of this process. This is important. No one can accuse you of personal political bias if you are acting on the basis of evidence, on behalf of, and with young people.

- Find colleagues who will act with you. If you act alone you can be isolated.
- Make sure that all your other work is up-to-date. Reports, returns, accounts, correspondence. You are exposed if your work is incomplete.
- Ensure that you have a record of good practice. Record your work. Send records of achievements to steering groups, management committees, and to the management team. It is hard to rubbish you or your work, if you have a good track record.
- Join a union.
- Get to know your organisation's policy and regulations about talking to the press, and approaching councillors, grievances, council members, or other policy and decision makers.
- Get to know the people in your organisation who may be involved with or interested in, the things that you are trying to achieve. Form a positive relationship, with them if you can. It is always easy to work from a relationship, even if you disagree.
- Be very clear what, if any, professional risks you are prepared to take, before you embark on any course of action. Stop when you get to this point.
- Be familiar with your organisation's disciplinary and grievance procedures.

It is to be hoped that you will not need to use any of these precautions, but you do not dig deep without this life saving equipment.

Case Study: A tale for youth workers

Les, a youth worker had an afternoon off and took it snoozing by a local river. There was a shout, and Les sat up and saw a young woman struggling in the water. Without hesitation, he dived in and pulled the youngster to the bank.

Scarcely had Les comforted her than there was another shout this time from a boy in the water. Les dived in again, and pulled him to the bank, and wrapped the two young people in his coat. Another shout went up: the tired worker swam across to a young man who was half drowned, and managed with his remaining strength to haul him to safety. The three young people and Les huddled together in an exhausted heap. A crowd had gathered near the bridge and applauded.

A voice shouted, 'Look, look there's another kid.' And sure enough someone else was drifting down in the current. The youth worker jumped up and started running up the bank. The crowd on the bridge shouted, 'Where are you going? The kid's there...'

Les continued to run upstream and the crowd on the bridge heard him shout, 'Someone else can sort that out, I'm going to get the bastards that are throwing them in.'

There are points in every youth worker's career when it is necessary to decide how much energy to use pulling young people out of the deep end, and how much they should expend preventing them from being thrown overboard in the first place.

Chapter Twenty-two

Steering Groups, Management Committees and Youth Forums

Some people think that management committees are a pain: I don't think like that. I see my management committee as a really useful group. They can speak on our behalf, support us. It's worth putting a bit of time into keeping them involved. People who get onto management committees are usually busy. They need to feel that it's worthwhile and that they make a difference. I try to do this by keeping them informed and inviting them to things. Yes, I see my committee as important.

(Project worker)

The management committee is a nightmare: they never turn up, and if they do they've never read their papers. We don't see them from one meeting to another. They wouldn't be seen dead in the places we work with young people. Our regulations say that we have to have them and I wish they didn't.

(Worker in charge: youth centre)

These are the two extremes of the views on management committees and steering groups. Most youth projects and clubs have to have a committee that oversees their work. Most youth workers will also agree that it is sensible to make these committees as **effective** as possible.

What Can a Management Committee or Steering Group Offer Youth Work?

It can offer:

- A place where people from different perspectives objectively review the work.
- A body to which the project is accountable.
- Ideas for problem solving and development.
- A link to other parts of the community, formal education, police, local residents.
- A supporting voice for the project.
- Opportunities for young people to practice representative skills in a real situation.
- A place where young people and older adults who would never usually meet can do so, and in the process may discover that their individual prejudices may be without foundation.
- Information and experience from wide ranging backgrounds.
- A range of different opinions can be voiced, otherwise these opinions might not be heard within youth work circles.
- Resources.
- Advocacy on behalf of young people.
- People who can become involved in the work on occasions:

 – Visiting the project.
 – Talking with young people and workers and becoming involved in formally recognising achievements.

Clearly the management committees and steering groups have potentially a great deal to offer. Then why is it that management committees and steering groups often do not meet their full potential?

The answer is frequently that for a variety of reasons, the youth workers do not put the time and effort into this area of work. The worker in charge is the best possible leader. It follows that each worker in charge needs to have a strategy for developing their committee or group, which must be achievable within the time constraints and consistent with the other areas of their work and the project's development plan.

Meeting the needs and wants of Committee Members

There are a number of ways that their **wants** and **needs** can be met:

1. Ensure that meetings are handled professionally, and that:
   - All papers are sent out on time.
   - Reports are short, clearly written and relevant. Always include a list of achievements since the last meeting.
   - If you want the committee or group to make a decision, then set out what the issue is. Also include the range of possible actions and a little about the advantages and disadvantages and the implications of each.
   - The meeting room is clean, warm, comfortable and well set out.
   - Refreshments are available and well presented.
   - Individuals are greeted appropriately.

   I've been to so many awful committee meetings. Papers given out on the day, people arriving as tables are shoved together, unheated rooms and coffee served in dirty chipped mugs. Yet workers then wonder why people don't want to be involved!   (Youth officer)

   It is worth giving thought to the form of the meeting:
   - Should it be formal, sitting round a table, or more informal in soft chairs?
   - Should the meeting stay together all the time, or should there be small groups looking at issues and reporting back to the whole meeting?
   - Should everyone be in the meeting all the time, or should different parts of the agenda be open to different people?

2. Phone members to ask if there is anything that they would like on the agenda, or if there is anything they want to ask. Discuss and explain any issues to them. Keep your chairperson informed about developments and problems and after meetings discuss the meeting with them.

3. Make meetings interesting with short presentations and discussions about wider issues.

4. Work with the young people who attend the meeting so that they know what to expect and how to make contributions. This may mean some training sessions. Could you involve some of the management committee or steering group in these?

5. It may be that the young people form part of a youth forum. In this case they will have definite items to raise and a body to whom they report. Build this into the political education strand of your work.

6. Take advice from the committee and acknowledge it. Don't just use the committee as a rubber stamp.

7. Keep networking: inform members of things that are happening. Send them newsletters or information about events.

8. If you have a display about your work, include names and photographs of the steering group or management committee.

9. Invite members to special events. Make a photo opportunity if this is possible. Involve young people in welcoming members and explain what is happening. This may require practice with role play beforehand, to develop their skills and confidence.

10. Work with the adults on the committee to ensure that the young people feel comfortable, enjoy it and contribute. Local politicians are sometimes willing to be involved in the development of young people as committee members even if they come from a different political perspective.

> *I'm not sure my party (Conservatives) would approve of me coaching potential young socialists: but it's so good to see them learning how to do it.*
>
> (Centre committee member)

You should now be in a position to draw up a strategic plan to develop the management committee or steering group. It may be that you find that you need new members. If this is the case you have an opportunity to involve any existing members in their selection and induction. Make sure that everyone knows:

- What the role of a member is.
- Expectations of them.
- The size of the committee.

When the strategy has been developed and put into action its success will depend initially on the enthusiasm, commitment and skills of the worker in charge. Gradually the committee or group should take on a life of its own. If this groundwork has been done well then you can move towards a situation where the group understands the work it oversees, and is committed to its success and development.

Youth Forums

Young people should be involved in all issues that concern them, because:

- They have a right, as part of the democratic process, to participate in decisions that affect them. They also need to develop a belief in that right.
- It offers a way of delivering the political education part of the youth work curriculum. It can also offer learning about:
  - power   – how formal meetings work
  - systems
- It also helps develop the skills of:
  - communication   – speaking in public

- making a presentation
- reading situations
- lobbying
- supporting others speaking in public
- representing others
- networking

There is a tendency for workers to seek to involve young people in a youth forum as their first experience of active participation. Involvement in youth forums needs young people to have quite advanced skills. They must be able to work on issues that are important to other people but not necessarily to themselves. Additionally, they must be committed over extended periods of time. Results are often slow.

This may be why workers have difficulty in getting a youth forum up and running. It might also be why they find that the most active members are older young people who have had experience in similar organisations such as school councils.

An alternative approach to developing participation is to establish a developmental pathway.

Developmental pathway: Stage One

Action research: where groups of friends deal with issues that concern them by:
- researching the matter
- carrying it out
- developing an action plan
- reviewing the outcome and their learning from it.

For example: campaigning for a BMX track, or tackling the management of a disco about bouncers who bully people.

Developmental pathway: Stage Two

Training: to support and develop young people in the skills of making their voices heard. The training needs to be active, fun and based on skill development through such methods as:
- role play
- assertiveness training
- case studies
- team building
- exploring issues through interviewing, conducting surveys, making films, writing short reports and press releases

If the training isn't enjoyable and relevant, young people will become bored.

When people first become involved in representation on a youth forum or management committee, there needs to be a high level of support. This means meeting with them before meetings and ensuring that they understand their role, the procedures, and how the meeting works, the agenda, and how important it is for them to work out how they feel about each item. They would also find it helpful to visit the meeting room, discover the toilets and where they can get something to drink.

When debriefing them after the meeting, discuss what happened, how they felt, what they learned, and what they need or want to do next.

As a tradition of representation grows, other young people with representational experience should be part of this process. These peer workers will need training and support in how to help and support someone new in the system, i.e. inducting them. Stage Two runs along side Stage Three.

Developmental pathway: Stage Three

Young people acting as representatives on Committees and groups: such groups include steering groups, management committees of current youth groups and planning groups for events in the locality. There are usually annual fun events, fetes and galas, water sports days etc. The planning committees are often pleased to welcome young people on to the main committee and to have sub-groups of young people taking responsibility for one particular aspect.

> *Our group tries to do something for the community activities every year. Last year we did the BBQ at the fireworks display and that lead onto doing traditional Christmas food at the Christmas charity fair. This year we aren't doing as much, because the people who were doing that have gone to university, though we are running a fun session for the 5–7 year olds in the Easter holidays... By the end of each year eight people will have been on the committee and twelve to fifteen will have taken part in the events.*

Developmental pathway: Stage Four

Once a pool is established of young people who have some experience of representing others and acting as peer workers, the activities of the young people may take on a life of their own, independent of youth workers.

Certainly these young people will have the skills to represent others in a wide range of situations and to campaign on their own and others' behalf. Young people in this category will never be token representatives. They will wish, and will be able to be involved in activities such as the appointment of staff, and the training and development of other young people.

> *...and before you say 'all that sounds very good but I bet it's just the few sixth formers who get involved in this'. No! it isn't, we've had some right scallys come through and come good. It's hard work, mind you. Two of the first bunch are parent governors now and one is a borough councillor. Two of the peer mentors went back to do their GCSEs and an introductory course on counselling. The sixth formers did take part but went off to college and have never come back to the area: by that token you could say that they haven't added to the strength of the community yet...*

This rolling programme of developing young people's participation, representation and political skills means that a youth forum should have a continual source of new membership. If it doesn't, the forum tends to have a 'stop, go' life, because groups of young people move away from youth work as they become older, or leave the area.

According to young people, youth forums are good when:
- *They aren't too cliquey.*
- *It feels OK to join in.*
- *Things are done, not just talked about.*
- *There's people who know what they are doing, not just everyone trying to find a way forward.*
- *It's really for young people, not because the youth workers' been told to do one.*
- *We have real power to do things.*

Youth workers would do well to listen to their views.

Chapter Twenty-three

Inter-agency Working

It is important to understand history, in order to make sense of the present, and make decisions for the future.

A Background to Inter-agency Working

Over the last 15 years the practice of inter-agency working has steadily increased. What have been the driving forces for this?

One of these has been the need to find a way of **engaging with young people** who are not succeeding in gaining qualifications or getting jobs. These young people see no hope of success in these areas, and little point in trying. They feel excluded, and often turn to the alternative economy for income and a way of life. Their lives become centred on benefits, petty crime, drug dealing and 'hanging out'. This group of young people have always been there and have been labelled in various ways. Their lifestyles have changed with the times and they have been variously called:

- Unattached, drop outs, in the 1960s.
- Disenfranchised, disenchanted in the 1970s.
- Disaffected, in the 1980s.
- Disappointed, excluded in the 1980s.
- Disengaged, in the 1990s.

In the 1980s there was a major change in employment. The silicon chip was developed, which made it possible to do many people's work with a single machine. There was **mass unemployment**. The industrial base changed from the heavy industries of coal, steel, shipbuilding and car manufacturing, to service ones. This caused further unemployment. The large number of young men without work were a social and political problem. The Governments of the day responded with a range of schemes such as community programmes, youth opportunities programmes, and 'New Deal'.

These schemes came from a mixture of purposes:

- **Training:** wanting to see young people gain the skills to become effective members of the current work force.
- **Control:** wanting to prevent the social unrest that was feared might result from mass unemployment.
- **Welfare:** wanting something 'better' for young people.
- **Economic:** people on benefits, and high crime levels, cost the tax payer money. High unemployment is very expensive to the nation.

The Governments wanted to get people into work to lower this cost. At the same time the ideas of financial control were being introduced: value for money, compulsory competitive tendering, cost effectiveness and best value along with quality assurance and quality control.

Not only was the Government trying to cut the cost of unemployment, it was seeking to lower the costs of the organisations working with the young unemployed. It became clear that there was a range of organisations and that:

- No single organisation has the 'right way' of working with disaffected young people: each has a specialist role. It follows that if two or more organisations come together they can offer more to young people.
- Young people in difficulty often find that several agencies are working with them:

– teachers	– social workers
– education welfare officers	– probation officers
– youth workers	– social inclusion teams
– youth offending teams	– specialist counselling and advice agencies

This is difficult for the young person, and it can lead to:

- Confusion between the different agencies, resulting in a lack of consistency for the young person.
- Time and effort wasted by the agencies as they duplicate each others' work.
- The young people playing individuals and agencies off against each other.

The New Labour government has promoted **joined up thinking**, where agencies work together in the best interests of young people. This has resulted in the establishment of:

- Youth Offending Teams.
- New Deal.
- The *Connexions* Service.

The latter employs people from different organisational backgrounds, and seeks to provide personal learning advisors who will work with the young people and other agencies to steer young people towards education, employment, or training.

Each of these organisations is concerned with inclusion, and with a specific area of young people's needs. As well as these national organisations, there are many local initiatives of two or three organisations working together, for example:

- Youth workers working in schools with young people who are on the edge of exclusion.
- Health authorities running multi-agency drug prevention projects.
- Voluntary agencies setting up multi-agency projects.

The way this point was reached is very logical. Each step followed the rest:

> *It's so logical and seductive. Why am I uneasy about the whole thing? Why do I feel that it's selling out young people? I suppose the proof of the pudding will be in the eating.*   (Very experienced part-time worker, on a difficult estate with high unemployment)

Clearly there are larger forces at work here. These will be taken up in the last chapter. This chapter deals with interagency working.

What are the Implications of this History for Youth Work and Youth Workers?

Inter-agency working will be with us for the foreseeable future, so almost all youth workers will at some point work alongside people in other agencies.

Which agencies can you work alongside?

In order to decide whether or not you can work with another agency you need:

- To be very clear why you came into youth work and what you see as the purpose of the work.
- To find out what are the purposes of the agency with which you might work, its:
  - training
  - education
  - control
  - welfare
  - economic reasons
- To discover something of their working practices.

If your views fit closely with the other agency's, then you will fit into the project well.

> *I enjoy working with Health Service people, they have opened my eyes to a whole different way of viewing health. It pervades every aspect of our lives and it has helped me to put some of my youth work in a context of ensuring young people are healthy, physically and mentally.*
>
> *They are easy to get on with, because we all want young people to grow up healthy. We all work on the basis that young people have choices and that all we can do is show them the options and hope that they will make sensible decisions.*
>
> (Youth worker in a drugs unit)
>
> *I've worked in the school for six months now, working with a teacher doing PHSE. It's never really gone well. We agree what we are going to do and that's fine. It's when we come to do it the problems start. She has a totally different style to me. She is always a teacher. She doesn't form close relationship with the kids like I do. She is always careful not to reveal anything of herself. I use what happened to me as a way of exploring things quite regularly. I could go on and on, we're just not on the same wave length. She uses put downs all the time: I don't agree with that.*

Only you can decide which agencies you can comfortably deal with.

Jenny Sayer (1984) researched teams of workers with young people. She found that teams which showed a common purpose communicated more accurately, and delivered work more effectively, than teams composed of a number of individuals with different purposes and beliefs. These factors cannot be ignored.

Managing your Boundaries in Inter-agency Working

When, for instance, three workers from different organisations come together, each comes with the culture and purposes of their own organisation, see Figure 22. In both Figures 22 and 23:

A: The inter-agency project.
B, C and D: The three different workers.
             The boundaries of the workers.

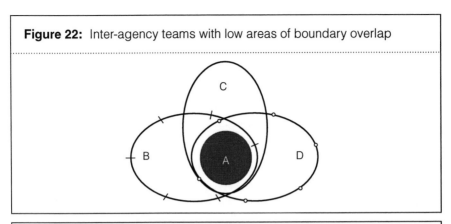

Figure 22: Inter-agency teams with low areas of boundary overlap

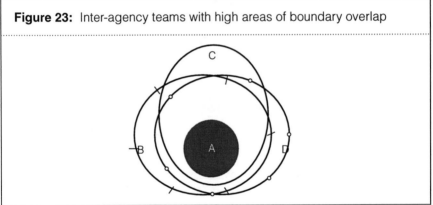

Figure 23: Inter-agency teams with high areas of boundary overlap

When a problem or an issue comes up in the project (A), each worker will bring their experience, and work culture, and beliefs to it.

If the boundary overlaps are small, as in Figure 22, then they may have problems. Imagine the difficulties, if worker B is concerned with growing and teaching young people, worker C wants to control young people, and worker D is only interested in welfare issues and drawing in funding from whatever possible source, to continue the work, or something like it, at whatever cost. This is a recipe for conflict.

On the other hand, if each of the three boundaries has large overlaps, as in Figure 23, then the three workers stand a good chance of becoming an effective team.

Before becoming a part of any inter-agency project or team, it is vital therefore to:

- Be clear about your own beliefs around work with young people.
- Understand the purpose of the project, which should be written in a policy statement.

- Talk with the other project workers and listen to their understandings and beliefs about the purpose of the project and how that should be put into practice.
- Enquire about how decisions are taken about fundamental matters in the project, work out where power is located, who has what power and what power you would have in reality.
- Find out about the funding of the project. Who will fund it? What are the requirements of the funders? What effects do these requirements have on the practice of the project?
- Read the inter-agency agreement or contract that sets out the details of the purpose of the project, its objectives, its procedures and practices, the timescale etc.
- Make sure that there is a framework of agreement which sets out practical details such as:
  - The name of the person in daily overall charge of the project.
  - The name of the person or body who is overall manager.
  - Who you report to, and how, and when you meet.
  - Who acts as cover, if the person that you report to is unavailable.
  - The limits of your authority.
  - How decisions are made in the project, and what voice you have in this.
- Where do they keep policies and regulations on:
  - health and safety   – staff development
  - child protection   – financial matters
  - fire
- Practical details of booking buses; hiring/using rooms/getting resources.
- Limitations on taking leave.

This may seem overly mechanistic, but it is far better to know the practical details of how the project works before a problem arises, than to have to work out an agreement in the middle of a problem.

Chapter Twenty-four

Conclusion

Anti-kipper Strategies and the Skills and Abilities Needed to Utilise Them...

This book has explored a number of **anti-kipper strategies** to help you stay an active and effective youth worker. All of these strategies require a common set of **skills** and **abilities** that include:

- The ability to think analytically, creatively and strategically.
- The skills of research through observation, listening to people and collecting data.
- Planning skills.
- Systematic working skills, those of identifying need, establishing an aim, setting objectives, devising work to meet these objectives, reviewing the work against indicators and the original objectives, and evaluation of all aspects of the work.
- The ability to build and maintain relationships with a wide range of people, policy- and decision-makers, managers, officials in other agencies, community members and above all, young people.
- Having and using high level interpersonal skills, including assertiveness and working towards a win-win situation in times of conflict.
- Recognising yourself as the major tool of your youth work delivery, and for this reason looking after yourself by ensuring that you have a support network, and by managing your boundaries and time, and thus reducing your stress.
- Recognising and developing your role as a manager and developer of staff.

Finally, we have defined youth work as being focused on **moving young people towards responsible autonomy**, helping them to take control of their own lives. It follows that the emphasis of our work is on the social, emotional and political development of young people.

The Purpose of Youth Work and the Need to Declare This

In previous chapters we have hinted that the **purpose** of youth work can bring youth workers into conflict with other agencies who see their role as the control, containment, welfare or training of young people.

The true purpose of youth work places young people and their agenda at the heart of our work. We need to be aware of agendas that other organisations have for two reasons:

1. Funding for youth work comes from Government, usually through the Local Education Authorities, who put their agenda into action by establishing funding

criteria that directs the work. Funding organisations such as the Lottery, and Comic Relief all have their own criteria for the disbursement of funding. There is no longer any such thing as funding without strings. Youth workers need to know what they are accepting with each funding source that they use.

2. In a world where inter-agency working is an expectation workers need to know their partners' agendas. They owe it to young people and their communities to declare openly and honestly the purpose of the youth work. If that purpose has changed as a result of different sources of funding, then it must be declared.

Social Inclusion as a Purpose

One of the common aims or bywords at the moment is that of **social inclusiveness**. This is a catch-all phrase that appears on the agendas of many organisations and can mean anything from:

- Enjoying the benefits of the freedom that comes with education, employment and money.
- Fitting in, and not being a drain on the state by requiring benefits, or taking up police resources or that of other agencies.
- Being a conforming, compliant member of the workforce, or recipient of education.

Before deciding that youth work is to be about social inclusion we need to declare the purpose of the work and consider the nature of society.

In whose world do we seek to include young people?

Each individual worker must make this choice based on their personal beliefs. It follows that everyone must be very clear about how they believe the world should be and what are the implications of this for their life, work and those who are close to them. There are many ways for an individual to live, many 'worlds' and 'societies' that are generally acceptable, and plenty that many people find unacceptable. Among societies of the twenty-first century are those of:

Sex, drugs, and rock and roll: the hedonistic, live-for-the-moment life style that exists in the pubs and clubs of towns and cities most weekends.

Rampant materialism: that stems from the belief that buying and owning things is of itself good, and that we can enrich our lives and be fulfilled by acquiring things for our immediate environment.

Ambition and being the best: here people set one particular goal above all else. Every aspect of their life is governed by their wish to excel.

Being middle of the road: having a job, but not being particularly well paid, having a family and children, not thinking too hard about anything and getting by most of the time.

Belonging to a faith group: and living out life based on its ethics and practices.

Belonging to a campaigning organisation: campaigning becomes the centre of your life. Such organisations include political parties, green organisations, animal welfare, etc.

Keeping up with the Jones: striving to do as well as your contemporaries in all things ranging from cleaners to children's achievements.

Being an active community member: being involved in the life of the community and its developments and issues.

Usually people do not live in just one world but combine two or three. It is however, rare to find anyone who has the time, or energy, to cope with more than this.

As a worker you must ask yourself what you are seeking to do for young people. Do you want to open doors so that they may choose which worlds to enter? If this is the case you must ensure that they have the skills, knowledge and attitudes that equip them to make this choice. Alternatively, are you helping them to acquire the skills and abilities to enter training and the world of work, but leaving them to decide their lifestyle without your intervention. Or are you directing young people towards a lifestyle and ethic base that you believe to be good and right?

When inclusion becomes part of your agenda, define its meaning for the young people and declare this. If you are working with another agency seek out their definition of inclusion, and then decide if the work that you are about to undertake is compatible with the purpose of youth work. Only then do you go ahead.

Young people's aims

Young people have their own agendas. These include:

- Making new friends and being with existing friends.
- Having a good time; having fun.
- Doing different and exciting things.
- Being valued and taken seriously.
- Doing things they see as bringing them into the adult world as equal adults. These may include drinking alcohol, using drugs, having sex, having a job, having and spending money.
- Having someone who is there for them at times of trouble.
- Being part of the current youth culture.

Unless we work in a way that takes account of young people's agendas they will vote with their feet.

Other organisations and their purpose

Schools, Colleges, New Deal, *Connexions* and employers all aim to ensure that young people are employable: only through employment can young people be included into the wider society. In practice this means being literate, numerate and IT competent with a predisposition to conform to the culture of the work place. A willingness to continue with training when in work is seen as a way to ensure the continued competitiveness of British industry.

The agenda of the Police, Juvenile Justice and other protection bodies is linked to developing law abiding citizens. It follows that they want to promote industry, conformity and diversionary activity.

Unless youth workers are seen to be sympathetic to these agendas, there is a danger the Youth Service will be marginalised, receive less funding or be directed to other work. There is a possibility that the Youth Service may cease to exist in its current form and youth workers may only be employed directly by other agencies who feel that their skills are helpful.

For these reasons it is more important than ever that youth workers can:
- Describe the purpose of their work and how they achieve this.
- Demonstrate its effectiveness from case studies, records, photographs and statistics.

When you are involved in inter-agency working negotiate to keep the youth work philosophy within the practice. Never rubbish others' standpoint, accept that it, like yours, has value. Neither standpoint should be lost.

A Youth Service for the Twenty-first Century?

The Youth Service has survived by making itself relevant to the context of young people's lives and remaining in touch with the national view of young people.

Following the Boer and First World Wars, uniformed organisations such as the Scouts and Guides recognised the need for discipline, self improvement, clean living, helping others and patriotism. During the same period Barnardos, the Boys Club movement, and the Girls Friendly Society all made an impact on dealing with the appalling poverty in which many young people lived.

After the Second World War the Youth Service responded to the needs of young people who had received reduced education and had little sense of direction beyond getting a job. Youth clubs were opened. Youth work took on an educational rather than a welfare role. Detached work expanded to reach 'unclubbable' young people. In the late seventies and eighties, Youth Work responded to the high levels of youth unemployment.

In this new century we must strive to work with the current context of young people's lives.

The current context

Young people in general are without direction and are ill-equipped for the world in which they find themselves (see Section One). They lack internal or external maps.

Mapping is the process by which all an individual's experiences, feelings and knowledge are lodged in their mind. These should be stored in a systematic way that allows the individual to:
- Make sense of their world.
- Recall parts at will.
- Fit new experiences into the existing map.
- Make comparisons and contrasts.
- Develop an ethical base and value code.
- Use past experience to help decision-making and planning.

Internal maps relate to:
- Feelings of self worth and self esteem.
- Understanding and valuing one's own emotions.
- Developing a sense of something greater than oneself, a spirituality.
- Enabling honest experience of feelings and thoughts.
- Providing a base for development of a shared language.

External mapping relates to:
- Understanding and recognising your location in the world.

- Coping with different situations by being able to understand the situation and respond appropriately (reading norms).
- Recognising the range of roles that young people play in different situations and why this is.

One youth work trainer summed it up thus:

> They are overloaded...I see it like this, they have hundreds of open jam pots of opportunity to choose from. Some are legal, others are illegal, but they have been created for the financial gain of the organisations...the organisations have no understanding of or interest in their value to young people or the effect they have on them...young people taste the jam because it looks good but they don't have anything to judge them against... They don't have an internal map or an external one and consequently their experience is fragmented. The nature of society makes it this way.

Groups swarm from one jam pot of experience to another because others say, 'hey, here's a good one'...experience for experience' sake, without pattern or coherence.

How can young people build up the maps when there is no-one to show them? Either the young people are left to their own devices and have no boundaries, or they are trapped by their parents' expectations, and limited by not being allowed to go anywhere alone. Often, there's no-one with the time to help them, neither family nor community nor schools. The media doesn't help either: they set people up and then tear them down, or sensationalise matters. The media offer non-stop stimulation with poor outcomes. How does this help to establish a map?

What young people need

What young people need, is to be helped to develop their own internal and external maps, so they know where they are and where they are going. If they had the maps they would be more secure.

It follows that youth workers need to offer a service that is:

- consistent
- coherent
- flexible
- stable
- responsive
- accountable

We must not lose our purpose of bringing many young people to responsible autonomy through caring positive relationships with youth workers.

We need to offer jam pots of experience in a way that helps young people to map their internal and external world. This means that we should offer a range of exciting and interesting activities and experiences, with young people participating in every stage of their organisation.

It is vital to review and evaluate the outcomes of these activities and experiences. This is the point at which young people's learning is consolidated in a way that enables mapping and their further development. Young people often say that they are 'bored. This way of working can fit with their agenda, and at the same time make them active participants in the organisation, thus moving them towards autonomy.

There is a huge range of agencies who work with young people. This often poses problems for young people who are trying to navigate their way through the system. Some are not very user-friendly, others do not help the young people explore the implication of the information that these agencies give them. The whole process of:

- Gathering accurate information.

- Understanding what it means and its implications.
- Making decisions based on the information.
- Putting the decision into action.

can be extremely difficult and stressful for young people: it is impossible without internal and external maps.

Young people need information services that help them through the information and decision-making process. Such services help with the internal and external mapping processes. Young people need to locate themselves in adult society. Involvement in such things as a youth forum, the millennium volunteers and the Duke of Edinburgh's Awards all provide experiences and frameworks for young people to use as mapping tools.

The internal map also requires a spiritual dimension. Thus, it is not necessarily to do with organised religion, but it is concerned with the location of humanity in the universe, each individual's understanding of what is right and what is wrong, the well-being of all living things on our planet. It is the element that is larger than self.

In good times it is something to celebrate; in bad times it is something to fall back on.

Youth work in the Twenty-first Century must refine its current curriculum to take account of these factors, see Figure 24.

The approach of reforming the Youth Work Curriculum, with an emphasis on the development of external and internal maps that enable young people to move towards responsible autonomy, should offer a service that:

- Is relevant to the agreed needs of young people.
- Is consistent with young people's agendas.

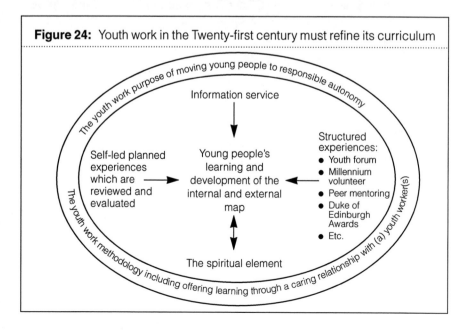

Figure 24: Youth work in the Twenty-first century must refine its curriculum

- Is demonstrably unique in its contribution to young people's development.
- Is consistent with high quality inter-agency work.
- Allows acknowledgement of other agencies' agendas.
- Provides a clear framework from which youth workers can negotiate the boundaries of their work.

This should avoid conflict.

And Finally...

The last section of this book has developed the ideas of the authors based on their current experiences of working in the Youth Service.

They are offered in the hope that you will explore the ideas, and use them as you will. Modify, accept, reject or build on them. Share your ideas with others, work to put your thoughts and analyses into practice.

Good luck! Stay rounded. Do not get kippered.

Acknowledgements

With grateful thanks to all those who have contributed through their work or significant conversations to the thinking behind the book, this includes:

Margaret Allen, ex-special needs advisor, Doncaster
Roz Bond, Senior Lecturer, Bradford College
Chris Brodhurst-Brown, Curriculum Development Worker, Doncaster Youth Service
Dave Churchill, Staff Development Officer, Doncaster Youth Service and NAYCEO
Carol Dunkerley, Youth Information Worker, Doncaster Youth Service
Dee Hammerson, Head of Doncaster Youth Service
Jen Jenkins, Area Worker, Doncaster Youth Service
Sandra Levington, ex-secretary, CYWU
Eileen Newman, Senior Lecturer, John Moores University
Keith Stewart, Brent Youth Action
Nalayini Thambar, University of Leeds Careers Service
Wyre District Youth Team, especially 'Mac'
Andrea Horscroft

References

Button, L. (1971). *Discovery and Experience*. Oxford: Oxford University Press.

Button, L. (1972). *Button's Continuum*. Unpublished, Swansea University.

Button, L. (1974). *Developmental Group Work with Adolescents*. London: University of London Press.

Ingram, G. (2001). Are You Being Kippered? *Young People Now.*.

Maslow, A.H. (1982). *Towards a Psychology of Being* (2nd Edn.). Reinold, Van Nost.

Pride, D. (1980). *From Communication to Personal Autonomy*. Bolton College of Education.

Pringle, M.K. (1980). *The Needs of Young People: A Personal Perspective*. Hutchinson.

Sayer, J. (1984).*How Does the Personal Ideology of the Community Worker Affect the Community Work Process?* Unpublished MPhil, Lancaster University.

Seyle, H. (1978). *The Stress of Life*. McGraw Hill.